Tevis Cup Magic

Taking on the World's Toughest 100 Mile Endurance Ride

HAPPY TRAILS LINDA!
Merri Melde

MERRI MELDE

• **The Equestrian Vagabond** •

Copyright © 2016 Merri Melde

All rights reserved. No part of this publication may be reproduced or transmitted in any form whatsoever or by any means, electronic or mechanical, including photocopy, recording, or any information storage and retrieval system, without permission in writing from the author.

Published by

The Equestrian Vagabond

Murphy, Idaho

www.TheEquestrianVagabond.com

Manufactured in the United States

ISBN-13: 978-0-9913460-0-4

DEDICATION

For Mia and Luca and Julian and Ellie

CONTENTS

	Acknowledgments	i
1	100 Miles One Day: The Tevis Cup	1
2	A Bizarre Twist – I Must Now Interview Myself!	5
3	Dithering	8
4	I Get By With a Little (Tevis) Help From My Friends	10
5	The Long and Winding Road to Tevis 2009	12
6	Getting Set for the Tevis Trail	16
7	2009 Tevis Cup – Phase I	25
8	2009 Tevis Cup – Phase II	41
9	2009 Tevis Cup – Phase III	57
10	Tevis Epilogue	74
11	Tevis Tutorial	79
12	Notes	83

ACKNOWLEDGMENTS

Thanks – as always – to the wonderful horses. You give us wings to fly!
Thank you Marsha Hayes, writer and editor extraordinaire, for your fabulous input and humor.
Thank you Nance and Bruce, and, of course, thank you Quinn for the great ride!

1: 100 Miles One Day: The Tevis Cup

It is not for the faint of heart: a hundred hard-won miles of rock, dust, elevation, uphill (19,000 cumulative feet of climbing), downhill (22,000 cumulative feet of descending), imposing mountains, plunging canyons, wild rivers, wilderness, extreme heat, suffocating humidity, extraordinary effort, and luck - good or bad, all in various doses, riding your horse across the Sierra Nevada mountains, in the dark and the light and the dark, all done within a 24 hour time limit. In 2010, Time magazine listed the Tevis Cup as one of the Top Ten Endurance Competitions in the world.

Starting at Robie Park near Truckee, California, and finishing in Auburn, California, the Western States Tevis trail follows a historic route of the Placer County Emigrant Road built in 1855, through the Granite Chief Wilderness, past historic mines and over old toll trails, and across the American River. Much of the trail traverses roadless and austere wilderness, reachable only by foot or horseback or helicopter, so for much of the ride, if anything untoward happens, you are on your own.

It's an arduous ride - to say the least - for a horse and rider. You and your horse can never relax or let up.

Discounting the two hour-hold vet checks, you have to keep on the move, steadily, for 100 miles, despite the rocks and bogs and cliffs and weather and fatigue and darkness. And no matter how good a rider you are, or how talented your horse is, you have only a little better than 50% chance of finishing the ride. If you do finish, it's likely that 50% of you will do so in the last 75 minutes.

It was 1955 when Wendell Robie set out to prove that any modern-day horse could traverse the rugged 100-mile trail from Truckee to Auburn in a single day. Since that first year when Robie and four other riders did just that (four of them finished), the 100 Miles One Day Tevis Cup has become an endurance institution in the United States. It's the ride against which all other 100-mile endurance rides are inevitably measured. It will top any bucket list survey among endurance riders around the world.

Despite the challenges, and despite the 50-50 chance of finishing, every year the riders come, for many reasons: for fun, for the challenge, for the beauty; to test their horse or themselves; to win, to finish, just to try; to conquer the trail, to conquer fear.

To truly understand the momentousness of this ride, you might contemplate the plight (or delight) of the Tevis Obsessed, those whose entire endurance season, and often, endurance career, revolves around this one ride every year.

It would be fair to say that Julie Suhr has been consumed by the Tevis trail. She has completed the ride 22 times in 28 attempts. She won her 2000-mile buckle, for 20 completions, with a still-healing broken collarbone on a borrowed horse. She finally, reluctantly, hung up her reins after one more attempt at the ride, at the age of 80. "My daughter pointed out that if I rode ONE MORE TIME, I'd have ridden in five different decades," Julie recalls. She was more than 90 miles into the ride when she pulled her horse. The horse was fit to go on. Julie was not. "I was not doing him justice," she said. One can imagine the courage it took to quit so close to the finish line. One can imagine the respect she had for her horse.

What one cannot imagine, unless also obsessed, is the pleasure she related at being out once again on the trail she loved. No bitterness. No regret. Just gratitude she rode those last 90 plus miles on a ride that ended in the moonlight, just three or four miles short of what some perceived as them "finish" line. To the obsessed, Tevis has no real philosophical finish line. It both refutes and reinforces the cliche about life is a journey, not a destination. Suhr understood this after decades of riding Tevis.

Julie's daughter Barbara White inherited the Tevis addiction gene. Barbara has completed Tevis a record 34 times in 45 starts through 2015. It is probably safe to assume that a week after Barbara's last finish, she was already starting to think about and plan for next year's Tevis.

Japanese businessman Seiichi Hasumi saw a documentary on television about the Tevis Cup in 2002 and decided he wanted to compete in it. He climbed on a horse for the first time in his life at age 59. The next year, he had his first Tevis buckle. He finished eight times in a row.

Donna Fitzgerald and her extraordinary freak of a horse, Witezarif, weren't just obsessed: they owned the Tevis trail for a while. In the 1970's, the pair won Tevis six times - four wins in a row, and they once finished second by one minute.

And on the other side of the Tevis trail, there's me.

Unlike most people who spend months, or years, preparing themselves and their horses for the great ride, Tevis was never on my radar. While I'd ridden several thousand AERC miles and completed two 100-mile rides over my 10-year endurance career, I'd never expected I'd get a chance to ride Tevis. I had never owned my own endurance horse (still haven't), and riding the Tevis simply never crossed my mind. I couldn't afford to lease a horse, and while it was not impossible, it was not easy to find someone to just give you a horse to ride in such an event. I wouldn't even think of asking, "Hey, can I ride your horse in the Tevis?" There was also the huge responsibility you had when you rode someone else's horse, especially on such a long and difficult ride. Tevis was so far off my feasibility radar it was never even an ambition.

I was conducting interviews for stories with some of the ride participants before the 2009 Tevis when Fate threw a four-leaf clover into the middle of my path.

2: A Bizarre Twist - I Must Now Interview Myself!

Monday before Tevis

My friend Nance Worman had arranged to loan her horse, Big Sky Quinn, to another friend to to ride in the 2009 Tevis. On Monday morning, with five days left till the ride, Tom backed out due to work conflicts. Nance called me and offered me Quinn to ride, as casually as she might have suggested meeting for lunch.

"*WHAT?!*" I yelled into the phone.

I was stunned with the offer. I'd just told someone the night before that I didn't have a burning desire to do Tevis, mostly because the opportunity to do it would be so slim, that I'd never thought much about it. "But of course," I said, and I quote, "if I were offered a horse, and I knew the horse was capable and fit for it, I probably would not say no." (How could one say no?!)

Quinn was in excellent shape. I had just watched Quinn and Nance finish an 80-mile ride in Oregon three weeks earlier. A bonus was that Quinn and Nance had finished Tevis in 2007, the first time for both, so they both knew the trail. I would be riding with Nance and her other horse Jasbo. I wasn't too worried about climbing on this horse I had never ridden - I had ridden *with* Nance and Quinn, and I was (pretty) sure he wouldn't buck me off.

Physically, I wasn't sure about *me*. Everybody who knew me knew well how I whined about the heat. I made jokes about it, but it wasn't just whining - I had a very hard time when the temperature hit 90 degrees. Tevis would be hotter than that. Heat stroke was a real possibility for me, and I just was not conditioned for extreme activity in the heat. I had been *avoiding* the summer heat, not exercising in it. If I ever rode Tevis, I would want it to be fun, not miserable (or worse); and high heat always made me miserable (or worse).

And there was my knee. It had been bothering me on and off for years, and pretty much constantly for the last year. Sometimes I could hardly walk for a while after a 50-mile ride, depending on the horse and the saddle. And I was suddenly tempted to ride for almost 24 hours on a new horse in an unfamiliar saddle? Was riding Tevis really worth the possibility of blowing out a knee? (Um... maybe...? What is the point of living in the modern age unless one takes advantages of the technology like knee replacements? Or IV fluids?)

And there was that little matter of the possibly broken toe from a week ago (I accidentally kicked a table), which I still could not comfortably get in a shoe and walk on, much less put in a shoe in a stirrup for 100 miles.

Ibuprofen would probably take care of the toe at this point, but nothing helped the knee. Pain wasn't *that* big of a deal, but the cost of fixing a destroyed knee - and the consequential time lost riding - was a big deal.

Another reality was the cost. Tevis is not inexpensive. Registering late added another $120 to the already-high $350 entry fee; of course I would have to have the silver Tevis buckle if I completed the ride, so that added $150 to the entry fee; I would have to buy a Cool vest to wear during the hot part of the ride or I'd die, just to name a few expenses. For that much money, I could ride at least six 50-mile rides, and I would hurt a lot less, and put real knee damage off longer.

TEVIS CUP MAGIC

Monday afternoon, I told Nance, "YES! Wait - NO!"
Any reasonable person in my situation would say no.

3: Dithering

Tuesday morning before Tevis

After a good night's sleep, and deep reflection on the pros and cons of riding Tevis, Tuesday morning I knew I'd made the right decision. I felt much better. I called Nance again. "Definitely NO. But thank you sooo much for the offer!"

Nance said, "OK, but you still have until tomorrow morning to change your mind!"

Then it happened: I went out that morning and had a great 12-mile ride on Jose, which made me start dreaming again, and think, surely I could eek out another 88 miles out of my body on the Tevis trail! And I called up Nance again and said, "YES! Wait - NO! Well – MAYBE!"

What was I thinking! I had less than four days to psyche myself up for the biggest ride of my life, figure out what I'd need, get it together physically and mentally, and I'd have to leave for California in two days.

Nance laughed at me. "Just let us know!" She and her husband Bruce would load either one or two horses in their trailer Wednesday morning and head for Robie Park.

I still had a day to decide. I alternated between

obsessing about Tevis till my stomach churned and my head hurt, and just trying not to think about it anymore at all.

4: I Get By With a Little (Tevis) Help From My Friends

Tuesday afternoon before Tevis

Try as I might to find some definitive sign that I should or should not do Tevis, nothing happened. There was no lightning bolt from the sky (that would have just ended it), no lucky feather from one of the six Ravens that landed in our tree Tuesday morning (I would have packed up and left for Tevis within the hour!), no chasm that opened up under my feet, no witch writing me a message with broom smoke in the Idaho sky, no deep Voice of God from the great void saying, "Ride, silly!"

I did hear a lot of friends' vocal opinions; and none of the cautionary woes that I mentioned made a dent in THEIR enthusiasm.

- "If your knee gets to hurting too bad, just have a horse step on your foot. Then you won't notice the knee anymore, or at least not as much. Once enough things start to hurt, you just keep on going. It's only for 24 hours, you can handle it." - from someone who rode with broken ribs

- "DO IT. Don't miss it - it's THE MOST BEAUTIFUL RIDE EVER!" - from a dirty old man with a knee problem

- "You were gonna buy the Cool vest ANYway" - from a fellow heat-challenged photographer

- "When you crest the top after High Camp, and see the mountains out ahead of you, THEN you will know why you said yes to the adventure." - Jonni in Texas

- "You will want to die the next morning, but it will be oh-so-worth-it!!" - Amanda in Idaho

I was presented with more sage advice: wear a Cool vest, a Cool bandana, and a Cool helmet liner. Stay hydrated. Take lots of good anti-inflammatory drugs for the knee. Ride vet check to vet check. One long-time endurance rider suggested, "Don't ride to the end of the trail, just ride around the next bend, or to the top of the next hill. You can always get that far." Looking at it that way, of course I could do that!

I got many, many email and phone best wishes and hugs and kisses. There was not one dissenting vote. Unanimously, the response was: GO FOR IT!

I was still hesitant; but in the end, it was Jose that carried me up to the home rim trail Tuesday morning on that awesome ride, my guru Kevin who pushed me to the edge of the precipice Tuesday noon when I talked to him on the phone for advice, and my hero Julie Suhr that kicked me over the top Tuesday afternoon when she answered my somewhat panicked email. Julie's words of encouragement brought tears to my eyes, including the final "And you can do it, Merri. I'll cheer for you at the finish line."

Of course I called Nance and said, "YES!"

5: The Long and Winding Road to Tevis 2009

Wednesday and Thursday before Tevis

My road to Tevis did not consist of any preparation. It was a very short path that did consist of second guessing, second thoughts, and a brief but healthy case of nerves.

I didn't give Nance a definitive "yes" until Tuesday evening. I didn't fax in my Tevis entry until Wednesday noon, and the Tevis office didn't get it, so *technically,* I did not officially enter Tevis until noon on Friday at Robie Park.

I spent Wednesday packing three weeks' worth of clothing and gear, everything I could think of possibly needing, for every kind of weather and circumstance, for the ride. Then I unpacked it all and re-packed it, to see if I really had everything.

The first panic attack came on Thursday when I was an hour into my nine hour drive from Idaho to Robie Park. "WHERE'S THE RAVEN?!" I couldn't do an endurance ride without my companion Raven puppet in my saddlebag, the Raven with whom I'd completed almost 3500 endurance miles together. I was not superstitious, but there was no way I'd ride Tevis without the Raven! I whipped off the highway, jumped out of my car and opened the trunk, threw things out of bags, into the air, onto the ground, and - hooray - there was the Raven, already packed into his saddle bag. Whew! First crisis averted.

Onward on the long hot drive from Idaho and into and through Oregon and its dreadfully boring 55 mile per hour speed limit, and across hotter Nevada. It was the perfect time to cram in my last minute heat training for the Tevis trail. In those five hours across Nevada, I drove in a car with no air conditioner, westward so the sun hit me full on, wearing a black Tshirt. I got stuck in road construction on Interstate 80 for a while under the blazing summer sun. I drove in a car with no working radio, which intensified the effect of the heat, since I had nothing to get my mind off it. And so I baked for hours, roasting my outsides and insides to quickly prepare for those hot, wind-less canyons I'd be riding through in two days.

This was serious stuff now. I wasn't just going to participate in the Tevis Cup. It was now THE TEVIS CUP. I was so grateful that I hadn't had the time for weeks or months to dwell on everything, to spend the energy psyching myself up, or psyching myself out.

I did, starting Monday, stop reading about scary trails and heat and bees, slickrock, dust, horses and people falling off cliffs, and my horse getting pulled at the Quarry vet check at 94 miles, six miles from the finish line. I stopped wondering about the price of and recovery time from knee surgery. I stopped reading about how to recognize and deal with heatstroke, and I stopped asking experienced riders how hot it was for them in the bottom of those canyons. I stopped asking people what and where exactly the worst and scariest parts of the trail were. I still wasn't sure exactly where "Pucker Point" was, and I no longer wanted to know, since I'd be riding over it. I wasn't afraid to die; I was afraid to get hurt again. And I was afraid of hurting somebody else's horse.

I figured by this point, being ignorant of what was ahead of me was a great advantage since I could do nothing to change it, so from Monday onward, I had pretty much ignored the entire possible sudden adventure until this long drive to Robie Park.

But once I reached Lake Tahoe and turned off Highway 267 onto the Mt Watson road leading along the ridge into the forest toward Robie Park, ridecamp for the start of Tevis, everything melted away. The mountains were stacked in blue and purple fading layers against the evening western sky, and covered with a pine forest that had just had a fresh rainfall (hailstorm, in fact). The Sierra Nevadas were my mountains. For nine years I'd ridden, explored, hiked, camped, climbed peaks, horse packed, and worked in these mountains and forests. Now they flowed in my blood, and I was coming back to do another endurance ride here. This just happened to be the Tevis Cup endurance ride, and I was coming to have fun and ride with friends; and however far I got down the trail (well, as long as I made it at least to Robinson Flat, at 36 miles), I'd be happy with everything I accomplished.

First thing I saw when I drove into ridecamp was friends and more friends. "I can't believe you're here!" "I can't believe you're riding!" (Neither could I!) "I'll be rooting for you!" "We just knew you'd say yes!" "You had to say yes!" "Good luck!" "You'll do great!" It all boosted my confidence and affirmed the rightness of my being here.

I spotted Far, my guru Kevin's horse, but Kevin, and friends Rusty and Bill, were off somewhere. Kevin was also riding Tevis. Kevin texted me later, "Are you coming over?" It was dark before I found them, and there were big hugs all around. Kevin was a wee bit nervous, but I was rather ecstatic to report that all my nerves were now gone - really gone!

Nance and Bruce were parked at the far end of camp,

next to fellow Idahoans the Yosts. Three of them would be riding Tevis this year. Chris Yost rode and finished Tevis in 2007 with Nance on Quinn. Chris was crewing for his wife Kara this year. Chris was more nervous than Kara. It was Kara and her horse Jack's first Tevis. Their daughter Laura was riding (she finished Tevis in 2006), and would be escorting her 13-year-old daughter Chandler on her first Tevis. Chandler would be riding the horse that finished with Laura in 2006. They were three generations of Yosts riding together. Laura's husband Gentry was crewing for those two. They gave me a yellow Team Endurance shirt to wear - I was an honorary Idaho Tevis endurance team rider for the weekend.

Nance's mount Jasbo and my mount Quinn had their noses buried in hay. It was a good thing to see: calm horses, eating well before a strenuous ride. We all visited, relaxed, ate, drank, did some minor rearranging and packing of our crew bags, enjoyed a blazing orange sky sunset, and went to bed early, to stock up on sleep for the long sleepless weekend coming up.

Just before falling asleep in my tent under the mountain stars in the cool air, I re-read the chapter "Pegasus" from Julie Suhr's book *Ten Feet Tall, Still*, her magical account of the Tevis ride. Her last paragraph of her victory lap at the finish in the stadium is simply magical:

"[My horse] breaks into a canter, and we cross the last few hundred feet of a hundred mile ride running. I jump off and wrap my arms around his neck as his sweet breath warms my cheek. I bury my face in the silky mane and the tears flow as they did in my childhood, not because the world has been unjust, but because it has been so very right. I had my Pegasus today. Together we reached the stars."

Will I ride my own Pegasus tomorrow?

6: Getting Set for the Tevis Trail

Friday, the day before Tevis

There really is nothing like waking from a good, deep sleep, outdoors in the pine and fir forests of the Sierra Nevada mountains. How could this not be a part of the good signs and good luck on this epic ride pointing toward the Auburn finish line?

I woke up before the others, when the sky was getting light, and crept around camp with my cameras, catching the calm before the Tevis storm. A few people were out walking their horses. Vendors were stirring. I stopped by Susan's Healthy as a Horse booth. I must have looked like a starving waif (possibly on purpose) because she made me coffee and fed me breakfast.

On the agenda today:

- Register for the ride (I could still back out!).

- Go for a ride, try out my horse Quinn for the first time, get acquainted very quickly, adjust his saddle to fit me.

- Fit my backup saddle to him that I brought along. In case my knee was killing me, I could switch saddles at Robinson Flat, at 36 miles.

- Pack food and clothing and whatever else I could imagine I might need for the two hour-long vet checks (Robinson, at 36 miles, and Foresthill, at 68 miles). Our crew would be meeting us at both stops with everything).

- Set aside my essentials for the morning: tights, shirts, Cool vest that Bruce loaned me to wear, Cool bandana for my neck, bandana for breathing through, gloves, chaps, helmet and helmet bandana, sunscreen, lots of lip chapstick.

My quick crash course in physical conditioning for Tevis included running back and forth all day from our campsite to Mansfield Arena, ridecamp central, at 7200 feet, lugging two camera bags, two big cameras, a little camera, another little bag, and a big jug of iced tea. This would hopefully quickly make me strong enough to drag my weary butt up into the saddle one more time at mile 94 on the Tevis Trail at approximately 3:31 AM, after approximately 22 hours and 16 minutes of riding, or thereabouts.

The Tevis Tension rate appeared to be comparable to the Tevis Completion rate: about 50%. About half the people wore smiles and half didn't smile or meet my eyes. I expected that had to do more with nerves than disappointment or unhappiness at being there. I knew, down the trail at some point, I would be tired and sore and sleepy, exhausted and fed up and maybe sick, possibly hurt or lost or disappointed. But now I really was having a good time at this endurance ride. I wondered if the frowning people were annoyed with me and my big smile?

A smorgasbord of horseflesh was assembled here for the ride: Arabians, Arabian crosses, a couple of mules, Morabs, Thoroughbreds, Pintos, a Mustang, a Kentucky Mountain Saddle Horse, a Paso Fino, and a Tennessee Walker. Riders from 18 states and four countries (Australia, Canada, England, Japan) were here. Anton Reid of Australia had loaned Christoph Schork from Utah one of his horses to ride in the Tom Quilty (Australia's equivalent of Tevis) a couple of years back, and Anton and Christoph tied for first place. Now Christoph was returning the favor by loaning Anton a horse. Seiichi Hasumi of Japan was returning for his sixth Tevis ride - so far he had an extraordinary record of five finishes in five starts.

There was already a line of people at registration when I got there at 10:00 AM. Those who were pre-registered were picking up their rider packets. I got sent to the back of the tent to Jo-Anne, who oversees the registration. "Oh yes, I remember you! Your faxed entry never arrived." She typed my information into the computer, but couldn't give me an entry number yet because her husband had driven off with her purse, which contained the thumb drive with the current registration information on it. (I could still back out!)

"Come back later to get your number," she told me. Jo-Anne put her head in her hands a few times that morning, trying to keep track of everything chaotic going on in there, but she was working very well under stress.

Every trip I made back to our camp, I spent some time packing. Or, rather, moving piles of things into different piles, thinking I would be needing them further down the trail. Let's see... full set of clothing change for Robinson and for Foresthill. No, wait, I'll put these tights in this bag, those tights in that bag. No, wait, I'll start off in these tights in the morning, put those in the Foresthill bag. But wait - will it be cooler or warmer tomorrow morning? How many layers should I start out with? I can't stand to be hot when I ride, and I had a feeling there wouldn't be much time to stop and strip and tie things to the saddle, or to stop and untie things from the saddle and put on layers on the trail. Maybe extra layers for the evening in case it got cold? What about rain gear - I have a rule to never go into the Sierra Nevada wilderness without rain gear.

When you ride only 50 miles, in several loops back to camp, you can get away with not having everything you need. Doing a 100-mile ride point to point, through some inaccessible wilderness, that would likely take me close to 24 hours, things would be a bit easier if I had everything readily available that I needed to stay a little more comfortable.

After going back to registration and getting my number - okay, it was official, no backing out now! - our Idaho team decided to go vet our horses in. Kara knew her horse would probably be calmer, and therefore have a lower pulse rate, if we vetted in before we went for a test ride. The 13 of us - five riders, five horses wearing their tack, and our crew members Bruce, Chris, and Gentry, paraded down to Mansfield arena and waited in line for our turns to go into the vet ring.

When our turn came, the veterinarian took Quinn's pulse, checked his hydration and muscle tone, and ran his hands down Quinn's legs to check for bumps or swelling. We trotted out across the arena to a cone and back to the vet, where he took Quinn's pulse again: "36" (very low!), and the vet scribe handed me back my vet card - we were now officially in the 2009 Tevis Cup!

Quinn got a big number 197 drawn with a grease pencil on each side of his butt, Bruce fastened my rider ID bracelet with emergency phone contact numbers on my wrist, and I weighed in with my saddle, hackamore, and horse boots - and now, we were officially, *really* in the 2009 Tevis Cup! Who would have thought it!

All five of our horses passed the vet-in: Team Idaho Endurance was in!

Back at the trailer, as we saddled up to go for a test ride, fellow endurance rider Karen Chaton appeared, taking photos and notes, and bearing a gift for me. It was a Tevis Guardian Angel. And it was made of glass!

"Put it in one of your saddlebags," she said. But it would break! "No it won't. I've carried mine through Tevis and across the country on the XP rides. She'll help you along the trail. Put her in the Raven bag!" So, in with the

Raven she went, my Tevis Guardian Angel, my two good-luck companions for the 100-mile journey on horseback tomorrow across the mountains from Robie Park to Auburn. My Raven bag was already strapped securely to my saddle.

We had just a short warm-up ride on the horses, down the road to the start and about a half mile further down the trail - exactly what we would do tomorrow morning in the dark. This was the extent of my "pre-riding the Tevis trail."

It took us a while to just get out of camp, because we kept running into people we had to stop and talk to, or to get off and hug. Endurance riding really is one big family. Nance and I finally got left behind when the other three gave up on us ever getting out of ridecamp!

We finally did get going, and had to pass a long line of horse trailers and cars stacked up one behind the other in a cloud of dust, still pouring into Robie Park. Once we got onto the real Tevis trail, Quinn and Jasbo did a bit of trotting, a bit of spooking, and Jasbo did a bit of almost-bucking when our friends passed us coming back. Quinn fed off Jasbo and was becoming a bit animated also, but once we turned around and got closer to ridecamp again, they calmed down.

I had to change my stirrup length a couple of times - I couldn't quite tell in that short jaunt which length was best, or which would be most comfortable and least offensive for my knee. I figured I probably wouldn't have time to jump off during the ride to adjust them, so I'd better get them right for the start! This was a treeless saddle, an unfamiliar one that put my legs out wider and more forward than I was used to. I detected a possible spot that might rub my skin just above my half-chaps, and I made a mental note to add either an ace bandage or vetwrap in my saddlebags, so that I could wrap my leg if my skin started to rub. Otherwise, that was all I could do, and I hoped I had everything right for a hundred miles of trail!

Back at our camp, it was back to packing: water bottles in the freezer - there's nothing ickier and less thirst-quenching than hot water to drink; mix up Gatorade, put those bottles in the freezer (and don't forget to move these to the ice chests in the morning!); food snacks in each crew bag; knee brace in each crew bag in case my knee was killing me; fanny pack in the Robinson crew bag, so I could carry two extra water bottles with me through those hot canyons between Robinson and Foresthill, in addition to the three bottles I was carrying on my saddle (Max told us he downed six bottles of water over that stretch in 2007); a little medicine bag for my saddle pack, with human electrolytes to help keep me hydrated, antibiotic cream, eyedrops, body glide (nothing worse than chafing for a hundred miles!), antihistamine for bee stings (I am not completely sure I am not allergic to them), Acetaminophen, Ibuprofen; a few snacks to carry on the trail in an extra little saddlebag; a syringe of electrolytes for Quinn; my vet card and checkpoint info card with the cut-off times; my little camera; and what about an Easy Boot in case we lose a shoe? It felt like I was packing for a two week trip, instead of 24 hours. I had no more room in my stuffed saddlebags. Did Nance have extra room?

What else could I be forgetting?

I still had to figure out what kind of food to bring tomorrow for the two hour-long vet checks. I remembered now, from the two 100-milers I rode six and seven years ago, that I did not like to eat during a 100, but eating was a must. What might I possibly be able to force down my throat that wouldn't make me nauseous?

I still had all the information in my rider packet to read - instructions on the start, vet checks and trail maps, what to do if your horse was pulled - but no time to read it all anyway. Tom had given us notes and time cheat sheets from his 2006 ride for us to study.

3:00 PM was the Mini-Clinic for first time riders. I'd

already missed the beginning of that, and, in keeping with my default strategy of ignorance, I was pretty sure I preferred to not know what they had to say!

There wasn't a whole lot in the way of planning strategy for the ride, except take it vet check by vet check. There were only two one-hour holds in the ride: Robinson Flat, at 36 miles, and Foresthill, at 68 miles. If you looked at it that way, Tevis was simply three "LD" rides - limited distance rides of 36, 32, and 32 miles. That made the ride sound completely feasible.

We were not in Tevis to try to win, nor to Top Ten. We just wanted to finish. In fact, we'd be riding our normal pace, which would put us at the back of the pack. Going by Nance's time last year, the first "LD" to Robinson Flat should take us around six hours. The second "LD" from Robinson to Foresthill should take us another eight hours - hopefully we would arrive around 8:00 PM. It was the toughest section of trail, with some wicked canyons - thousands of feet of ups and downs and the highest temperatures of the ride - along the way. If we were lucky enough to make it that far, we were two-thirds done with the ride! Only one more "LD" to go: 32 miles to the finish, about eight hours of riding, all of it in the dark. That, including the two hour-hold vet checks, would put us close to the 24 time limit.

There were seven other vet checks scattered along the trail, but they were all "trot-by" or "gate and go" stops: once your horse passed the vet check parameters, you could continue on the trail. You could stop and let your horse rest and eat, but with the time clock always relentlessly ticking - and those statistics of half the finishers coming to the finish line in the last hour and 15 minutes of the ride - you didn't want to waste time anywhere on the trail.

We skipped the big ride dinner, but we stopped what we were doing to go down to the all-important Pre-Ride meeting at 7:00 PM.

TEVIS CUP MAGIC

This year I'd lucked out: it was possibly going to be the coolest Tevis on record, though "cool" and "hot" is a relative term, interpreted very differently by different people. And there was nowhere close to the limit of 250 riders. If I'd get nervous about anything, it would be milling around with 168 other swirling, anxious horses in the morning waiting to crowd onto the single-track trail.

Although I'd previously never had a fervent wish to do Tevis, mostly because I just never imagined I'd have the opportunity fall into my lap, now that the stars had aligned and it was here, thanks to Nance and Bruce, by God, I really wanted to finish. Of course everybody wanted to finish Tevis, for their own particular all-consuming reasons, but my motivation trumped everything: this year's Tevis ride was dedicated to Julie Suhr.

Julie is my hero, my inspiration. I am in awe of her, what she has done, what she still does, the way she writes, the way she encourages, the kind of human being she is. And when it was announced that Julie would be handing out buckles to the finishers on Sunday, well that about did me in.

Imagining Julie handing me a hallowed silver Tevis buckle, *me,* who never expected to have the privilege of trying the Tevis, well, that squeezed my insides and choked me up. I didn't know if I would help or hurt my chances by thinking ahead to Sunday around noon where Julie would slip a buckle into my hands, and say "You did it!" or if I should not even think that far ahead. Was it good luck to think positively? Or was it bad luck to be cocky? I didn't know the Tevis Gods or what they preferred. So I did both - thought about it a little and totally tried not to think about the finish at all, because it was a long journey away, many aspects of which I did not have complete control over.

The meeting ended efficiently after an hour, and people departed in the twilight with hugs and good luck wishes. Nobody knew exactly what was ahead of them on the trail tomorrow, other than, no matter who you were, or how good you or your horse were, half would be lucky tomorrow, and half would not.

It was getting close to dark, but we still had work to do back at the trailer: last minute equipment checking and adjusting, last minute bag packing. We still had to mix electrolytes with probiotics in applesauce for the horses. Some of it went in each Robinson/Foresthill vet check bag. A bottle went in our saddlebags for the stops on the trail in between. Nance liked to dose her horses with electrolytes along the trail any time they took a good drink. We mixed more for one dose tonight before bed, and one dose tomorrow morning.

We walked the horses around camp once more to loosen them up, fed them more grain and hay.... then it was near 11:00 PM and time to get to bed and try to get some elusive sleep for the long journey ahead in the morning. The day had flown by; if I'd have any nerves, there would have been no time to get nervous anyway.

We set our alarms for the ungodly hour of 3:30 AM for the 5:15 AM start.

7: 2009 Tevis Cup - Phase I

The "first LD":

• Robie Park to Squaw High Camp - 13 miles - Water stop only
• Squaw High Camp to Lyon Ridge - 8.5 miles - Trot-By
• Lyon Ridge to Red Star Ridge - 7 miles - Gate and Go
• Red Star Ridge to Robinson Flat - 7.5 miles - 1 hour hold at 36 miles

    The best Tevis advice I'd been given was by friends who'd finished: ride vet check to vet check. With only two one-hour hold vet checks, Robinson Flat at 36 miles, and Foresthill at 68 miles, that divided the ride into manageable portions, and made it look doable. The start was at 5:15 AM; I figured we could plan on finishing (if we were so lucky) around 4:45 AM, 23 1/2 hours from then, if we went the same pace that Nance and Quinn did when they finished in 2007.
    But I wasn't able to think much of anything when I woke up before my alarm at 3:20 AM (not that I slept much), because I could not get my s*** together. I had made a pile of my clothing to grab and put on, but when

the alarm went off I could *not* find my tights. They weren't on the pile, they weren't in the bag, they weren't in my bed (the table/bed in Bruce and Nance's horse trailer), and they weren't on the floor. Tevis Gremlins obviously hid them. I must have wasted five minutes fumbling around for them. I finally had to go dig a whole new pair out of my duffel bag. Then I couldn't figure out what to eat, or how to make coffee, something I'd been doing pretty much all my life.

When it came time to saddle up Quinn in the dark, I could not get the saddle to fit right. It had fit just *fine* yesterday, but now the breast collar was too tight, *and* the crupper under his tail was too tight. This was not mechanically possible, but this is how it was at 4 AM. I had to loosen both the breast collar and crupper, which did not make sense... and I knew that not far down the trail they would both be too loose and I would have to stop and adjust them.

Then, I could not get Quinn's front brushing boots on - they were brand new, and the three dang velcro pieces on each boot kept sticking back to themselves before I could slip them through the buckle. I spent five minutes just on those front boots! Fortunately, Quinn just stood there stuffing his face with hay while he waited for my fingers to finish fumbling.

I double checked the Raven bag, with the Raven and the Tevis Guardian Angel inside, assuring it was cinched down tight, and that the two were getting along. I didn't want to have to backtrack a hundred miles of Tevis trail looking for a lost Raven!

Finally we were ready to head for the start. I had to pull Quinn's head out of the hay bag. That was a good sign - he was tanking up for the long day! As Nance and I waited for our three Idaho friends in the blackness, I got one little twinge of nervousness. Oh, this would not do! I tried to remember this ride was no big deal, just a ride starting way too early for my taste, and repeated to myself,

TEVIS CUP MAGIC

This is just another endurance ride, just another endurance ride. And miraculously, that anxious spasm went away. I must have forgotten about Julie Suhr and the finish line.

Our crew followed us with flashlights in the dark to pen two. The field of entrants was divided into two pens; the faster horses and riders would start out of pen one. We knew we'd be riding slower and toward the rear of the pack, so we started from the second pen. We were relieved that our horses waited calmly.

Someone yelled it was time to start walking up the road, and we headed out of our pen, following other horses in the dark to the road toward the starting line. We called out our numbers to volunteers with flashlights and clipboards as we left camp, escorted by claps and cheers from onlookers, and those magical words, "See you in Auburn!"

The 10 minute walk down the road to the official starting line became a 300 yard trot - then a 10 minute stand-still as the 150 horses ahead of us funneled onto the two-track trail. Unbelievably, our horses, and all the horses around us stood quietly. Kara's horse Jack posed like a model, legs straight, toes slightly pointed daintily outward, his head bowed, looking out from under his eyelashes, as if he were in a halter show. But he was no prissy horse. Nance called him the "Energizer Bunny," and he'd be zooming along the trail later in the day ahead of us so that all we saw of him at times was his dust.

Finally, the mass of horseflesh started moving again. Gradually we reached the starting line where we channeled off the main road onto the two-track trail - and we were off on our colossal Tevis adventure!

I can sum up the first phase of the Tevis Trail in two words: ROCKS and DUST. Not that there weren't rocks on the trail for a hundred miles, but there were a lot of rocks underfoot along this stretch. A. Lot. Of. Rocks. Granite Chief Wilderness. *Granite*.

And Dust - pervasive, invasive dust, and as the day

went on, horrible, torturous dust.

The dirt road we started on was a wide two-track that eventually narrowed to a single track. There wasn't too much passing or pushing or shoving going on in our surrounding bubble of horses. Nobody's horses balked at the little ditches we went over, nobody got bucked off, and nobody yelled too much. It was a very orderly start considering all the horses, around us anyway, something which I heard does not always happen, and something I had been a bit worried about. We five Idaho Spuds even managed to stay right behind each other.

The line of horses - 169 horses long - moved along at a good trot. Usually in such a long line, you have the annoying accordion stops that squeeze back down the line and you'd trot-stop-trot-stop; but a slight sense of urgency remarkably kept the whole line moving at a good clip most of the time.

The trail twisted through the forest, along the side of a mountain, up and down and around, but mostly down, six miles to the Truckee River. Once in a while the trail would widen to a two-track, where some anxious people would sprint ahead, only to cause a jam up with everybody trying to funnel back down to single track. If your horse slowed to a walk anywhere, like, say, when your horse put his head down to negotiate some tricky rocks, or when the horses in front of him slowed down, you might get yelled at by, say, the one guy behind us who was impatient and perhaps should have started closer to the front part of pen two. He would sigh *very loudly and pointedly* behind me - as if I could do anything about the long line of horses in front of me.

Much of the Tevis trail was like this - long single-track - where there was no place for anybody to pass. You could go on for miles behind, or in, or in front of, a string of horses, and you went with the flow of traffic, and if you didn't like it, you lumped it. It's just the luck of the Tevis draw, whether you were in a line of horses, or if you had a nice bubble to yourselves. We often found ourselves in a line during the day and night, particularly on the last phase.

As we zipped along, I was adjusting to Quinn and his modus operandi; he was adjusting to me. He liked to be right on Jasbo's butt - where he couldn't see the rocks his feet were landing on - and I preferred him to be back a little bit so he could see where to put his feet. We eventually worked out a compromise, but it took a while, and we did some stumbles, though I'm sure every horse was doing that in the excitement during the beginning of the ride. Fortunately Quinn was smooth, and though the sports saddle and my position in it felt unfamiliar, it was comfortable. And, so far, with 94 miles to go, my knee was not screaming!

This area was slightly damp from the rain/hailstorm/thunderstorm that hit Robie Park on Thursday, but you could tell the boundary of that rain, because it quickly became dusty.

Ah... the dust. What would eventually become for me a major bane of Tevis was just beginning. I could imagine a long snaking line of dust being kicked up, that could possibly be seen from outer space. It was like a creature, rising and writhing up from the earth then hanging there. From the couple hundred hooves in front of us, already the dust reached over the tops of the mature fir trees like a heavy cloud of fog. Fortunately I'd worn a bandana just for breathing in, and I whipped that over my mouth and started using it right away.

Down at the Truckee River, we crossed under the highway, and here were three members of my fan club. Crysta, and my adopted uncle and aunt, Dick and Carolyn, cheered when they saw me - all 10 seconds of it. Carolyn had a Cool vest for me to grab and put on just in case I'd need one for the hot canyons ahead, but I yelled that I had one. We didn't hesitate but flew onward, calling out our numbers to volunteer number-takers, me waving over my shoulder like a queen of the Tevis procession, as the little crowd of spectators cheered everybody on.

Trotting along fast, flying over the rocks hidden by fine silty dust, we dropped down to the Squaw Valley ski area, onto a nice easy dirt road, where, still in a long line of people, I noticed that the trail veered to the left off the road. Our group of five had just passed by yellow turn ribbons and over a white line across the road that indicated plainly, "Don't go this way!" It gets easy just to follow people robotically - which over a dozen riders had already done, going far around the corner and on down the road.

I yelled, "Wrong way! Hey guys! Trail goes off this way!" I pulled back to let those behind me take the trail first, and to wait for my Idaho Spuds (Quinn and I were ensconced comfortably in the rear of our group of five). As they turned around and came back, Mr Crabapple - who hadn't even noticed he'd blown by the turn - followed the redirected riders and spat caustically, "Well I guess that's what the yellow ribbons are for!" We made sure he passed us so he could go bite someone else's head off.

Back to flying at a fast trot along the dusty, rocky trail (I may as well now just drop the "dusty" and "rocky" descriptions - how about if from now on I mention if the trail suddenly was NOT dusty or rocky), on a steep slope, Laura was in the lead, when her horse hit some slickrock, and fell right down.

It happened so fast, none of us even let out a peep; we just slammed on the brakes to keep from running over them. El Din's feet whipped out from under him to the downslope, and Laura sort of fell off into the upslope; El Din was able to scramble right back up, and he stood there while Laura jumped back on. And quick as that, we were back scooting along at a trot. When something happens, if there are no injuries, you just keep going, because you quickly have a line up of riders behind you that you don't want to hold up.

From Squaw Valley the trail climbs 2500 feet amongst the ski lifts toward Watson Monument at 8774 feet, which honors Robert Montgomery Watson, the pioneer horseman who helped finish marking the Emigrant Road - now known as the Western States Trail - from Tahoe to Auburn in 1931. Less than a mile from the very top, there was a water stop at High Camp. Quinn and Jasbo didn't want any water. It was only 13 miles into the ride, and it was still cool, but we sure would have been happier if our horses took a drink now, with 87 miles ahead of us. Quinn didn't want any grass either, and Nance said he was a good eater. Hmmm. I didn't like that.

Something to file away and worry about later, but not yet, because my horse was feeling awfully strong. He was more interested in jigging than walking, so we trotted quite a bit of the uphill pulls. Some guy in front of us got off to walk the last steepest part: admirable! That's one thing I knew I wouldn't be doing. I might get off to walk some downhills, but for the rest, Quinn would be carrying me. I was too out of shape to walk uphills fast at altitude, and I won't tail a horse, since I permanently carry 7 plates and 21 screws and scars in my face from a hoof in the mouth 10 years ago. But that's another story.

We crested the climb at the Monument atop Emigrant Pass, at 8700 feet the highest point of the trail, our horses huffing steam from their noses in the cool morning. Shiny blue Lake Tahoe gleamed in the east as the golden sunrise hit the water, and the Granite Chief Wilderness sprawled before us to the west. Looking ahead from that high perch, I strongly felt the pull of Wendell Robie's 54-year-old challenge, and for the first time I did indeed know, with no reservations, that I belonged here in the saddle on this adventure today.

From here to Robinson Flat, our trail mostly followed the historic route of the Emigrant Road. Sure made you feel for those emigrants! Ahead in our path lay the Granite Chief Wilderness, and some real Rocks. They don't call it Granite for nothing. Jasbo was wearing four brushing boots on his legs for the first time ever, just because of this section. Quinn was wearing four boots just for this section. Miles and miles of rock to negotiate: leg twisting rocks, rocks hidden under dust, slippery rocks in streams to tumble over, rocks hidden in the infamous bogs, (the bogs were supposedly not so bad this year), rocks to just plain knock you down or shred your skin or break your bones if you happened to hit them.

Sometimes we plowed through tunnels of overgrown willows, so thick it was almost dark, so low I'd lean over my horse's neck to get through, as he picked his footing over the rocks, always the rocks.

When you didn't walk, you had to trot as fast as you could - over rocks. There's no dilly dallying on this trail. You have to constantly keep moving, keep pushing, though your speed limit is dictated by the terrain.

To our left a wide and deep canyon yawned, with granite rock faces thrusting up imposingly out of thick forests. I mostly kept my eyes on the trail though - when I could see through the dust - and both hands on the reins, ready to yank Quinn's head up when he tripped at our fast trot. When we had to walk, I gave him his head because he was usually very good at picking the best way through the perilous footing without any advice from me.

I'd been concentrating on Quinn's footing and my balance with him when I looked down and saw that his saddle pad was slipping back! The left side was already completely under the front of the saddle, and there was just a quarter inch sticking out on the right side. It had taken me this long to notice it - what kind of experienced endurance rider was I?!

I hollered that we'd have to stop at some point so I could readjust the saddle pad, and Nance said she'd take Jasbo's boots off. She thought we'd be out of the worst of the rocky bogs in the wilderness soon. Right now there really was no place to pull over - people on our tail and nothing but rock slopes above on one side of us and below on the other side. After a few more miles I called, "I really have to stop now!" because I could picture the saddle pad flying out from under the back of the saddle, and me arriving at Robinson like a wingding without my saddle pad. I had wondered before how on earth somebody wouldn't notice their saddle pad flying out from behind the saddle - and it almost happened to me here!

Laura came to a place that had only a tiny bit of room for the five of us on a slope and pulled over, and I jumped off and quickly loosened my girth. It was almost impossible to pull that danged heavy, wet-with-sweat pad, forward underneath that saddle without taking the whole shebang off. It was in actuality light, but seemed to weigh 400 pounds already. I ran from one side of Quinn to the other, two or three times, heaving and grunting and cursing at it - I frantically felt the minutes ticking away - before I finally got the pad pulled forward enough. I quickly tightened the girth, and snugged up the crupper a notch, and hopped back in the saddle, panting with the exertion, but Nance still wasn't quite done with getting Jasbo's boots off, because he didn't want to stand still.

Three riders were coming up behind us, fast, and zoomed past, calling "Are you alright?" Not that they'd stop to help unless we were dying - because you had to keep moving. We'd have done the same thing, asking but hoping they didn't need any help - and in fact we already had done the same thing, flying by a group dismounted and trying to put on an Easyboot on a horse who'd lost a shoe.

As soon as Nance was finished, she hopped back on, and we five were quickly flying down the trail again, trying to make up for those precious minutes we'd lost there.

We said goodbye to the Granite Chief, and the rocky footing improved slightly, although "slightly" is a relative term. The trail continued up and down to Lyon Ridge - a trot-by vet check, where the chaos of horses swillering around the water troughs and flakes of hay left me dazed.

Nance and I stopped right at a water trough - our

horses didn't want a drink - and then we jumped off to electrolyte them, but we didn't have our system down yet and we lost time. Nance pulled out the bottle of electrolytes and an empty syringe from a saddle bag; Quinn and Jasbo about knocked us both over trying to scratch their terribly itchy heads on us; between us we couldn't siphon enough electrolytes out of the bottle because the syringe was sticky; Quinn clamped his mouth shut for his dose; Nance tried to fill the contrary syringe then electrolyte Jasbo; I was trying not to get run into by another horse's butt; Nance lost the lid to the electrolyte bottle and we looked and looked but couldn't find it in the mud beneath our feet; I shoved her syringe in one of my bags while she shoved the open bottle of electrolytes in her bag and we jumped back on our horses looking for Kara, Laura, and Chandler, but didn't see them and we pushed and shoved our horses through the seething mass of horses and riders and took off. Quinn and Jasbo may have had a slight breather, but I was winded!

The vets waved us onward as we trotted by them out of the vet check. We weren't sure where our other Idaho Spuds were, but there was nothing to do but continue trotting hard on down the trail. The famous Cougar Rock was coming up soon. Nance called over her shoulder, "Are you going up?"

I said, "I'm following you! (I was riding Nance's horse; I was doing what she was doing!) What are you doing?"

"I'm going around. I'd rather finish the ride than get an awesome picture."

"Me too!"

As we approached the imposing rocky crag, we caught sight of three yellow shirts just cresting the top of Cougar Rock - several photographers standing on it shooting from different angles, and a line of horses standing impatiently and waiting to go over it one at a time - and we zipped around the side of the cliff, by chance ending up right behind our companions on the other side.

The trail followed a very scenic ridge, with deep plunging canyons on both sides of us. We came to a section called the Elephant's Trunk, a slight dip then a very steep, sharp curving incline over loose lava rock with a bottomless drop-off on one side. Our horses puffed hard as they climbed. Then we swooped down into the forest, back into heavy silty dust, and tripping rocks underfoot. The dust stretched to the heavens and hung heavy in the air. My dust-scratched eyes protested the thickness. The tears I blinked turned to mud that ran down my cheeks.

Quinn followed the others, stumbling, coughing, plowing through the rocks and dust. Great ethereal light for shooting photos, but I left my little camera in its bag and held onto the reins firmly with both hands to steady my horse, and gasped through my bandana.

We had a respite for a few miles over a logging road - dusty, but not so rocky - coming into Red Star Ridge, at 28.5 miles, our first gate and go vet check. If your horse's pulse was already down to 60, you could breeze right in, get his pulse taken, go straight to the vet, and continue onward.

Once again there was a big cluster of horses here; one of the volunteers with a stethoscope took on our group of five. Quinn finally took a drink - not a big one, but a drink, and we sponged the horses off to cool them down and bring down their pulses, and pulled over to the side where they dove at some hay. Another volunteer filled our water bottles. The heart rates of Quinn, and Kara's horse Jack, just would not come down to the pulse criteria of 60. The volunteer took Quinn's pulse again, we sponged him, took the pulse again, sponged him, and did it again. He was hanging around 64, and it probably didn't help that he was eating (which raised the heart rate slightly) - but he was so hungry, which was the lesser evil I wondered? Let him eat because he's starving because the fuel will help him down the trail, or make him stand there and not eat till his pulse is down?

I walked Quinn back to a water trough amidst all the other horses but he didn't drink. Another volunteer there took Quinn's pulse, and said it was 80. 80! I knew that couldn't be right, so I went back to our own volunteer and companions. She still got him at 64. *Come on Quinn, you've got to pulse down!* We were losing time here. More sponging with cool water. It worried me a little bit - it wasn't the hot part of the day yet, and Quinn's pulse was running a little high.

Finally, both Jack and Quinn were pronounced to be at 60. We moved on to the vet, and fortunately didn't have to wait in line there. A quick overall check, and trot out one direction - "Okay! You're good! Keep going!" - and we mounted up and kept going down the road.

We left Red Star 15 minutes after we'd arrived - and were far enough at the back of the Tevis pack that several of the vets were now leaving and heading to Robinson Flat. It was three vets in three vehicles to be exact, because we got completely dusted out by each of their trucks. "Sorry about the dust!" they each yelled. If only they knew! What could I do about this? Beat up a Tevis vet? That would be bad form, so instead I just laughed, and kept trotting along on my wonderful horse and breathing through my bandana.

As we fast-trotted along, Nance pulled out Tom's cut-off time notes that he'd given us. Robinson Flat - the first hour hold - was seven and a half miles away. Tom had arrived there at 11:18 AM. Recommended arrival time was 11:00 AM. The cut-off time was 12:00 PM. We looked at our watches. If we were lucky, we might hit Robinson around 11:20.

We played leapfrog with Bruce, from Arizona, on his Tennessee Walker, John Henry. This was Bruce's sixth Tevis, trying for his first completion. Bruce had on an awfully clean white long-sleeved shirt - how did he manage that! My borrowed light yellow long-sleeved Idaho shirt was already a light shade of gray. "Hey Bruce - how come you look so CLEAN?" It wasn't just blackened clothes we had on, but our faces. Nance and I cracked up at the dirt/mud smeared around our glasses.

We seemed to be absolutely flying along at a trot. 15 miles per hour it felt like, though surely I was exaggerating in my head. I was slightly worried about Quinn's pulse taking so long to come down at Red Star, and was wondering if we were going too fast for him; but, he was pulling on me, and Nance didn't say anything about his speed, and she knew how fast they went in 2007, and Jasbo was keeping up or pulling ahead of us.

And anyway, we had to keep pushing. If we arrived at Robinson at 11:20, we were only 40 minutes ahead of cut-off time! It seemed impossible to be cutting it that closely, because we seemed to be moving so fast!

I'd settled into a comfortable rhythm with Quinn, finding myself breathing in time with his pace, balancing over his center as he negotiated rocks in the trail, sometimes slightly shifting my weight just before a foot fell as if we were precisely placing the foot down together.

"Anything special I need to know about Quinn?" I had asked Nance yesterday.

"Well, last year at Deadwood (at 55 miles), he laid down at the vet check." He what!?

"He ran up that steep canyon, and at the top, at the vet check, he just laid down. He wasn't colicking, and he wasn't hurting, he just laid down because he was tired - stretched out like a cat, and laid there and ate a while." A vet kept an eye on them - Nance told him that Quinn had done it one or two times before - but Quinn apparently was just resting. When it was time to go, he got up, they went on, and they finished Tevis (and the other rides he'd laid down in.) We debated on this stretch if Quinn would lay down today. I hoped for my heart attack's sake that Quinn didn't do it today!

We had a little break from the dust here on this two-track road; my knee wasn't hurting; it wasn't too hot yet; I was having fun with my Tevis horse Quinn; and all of a sudden, we came upon a pink sign: "Robinson 4 miles." Whoops and hollers from us, and the horses picked up the pace. Quinn was on a mission, because he knew lunch was ahead!

"Robinson 3 miles" then "2 miles," then "1 mile," followed by signs, "No crewing this side," and a glimpse of a horse trailer through the trees: we had arrived at Robinson Flat!

We had arrived in Chaos Central, is where we were. Gobs of people, horses, crews, more people, horses squeezing in beside each other at water troughs, horse butts in your face, horses knocking into you - Quinn didn't drink - no sponge handy to splash him down - one sponge between Nance and me, and Bruce had it in his hand when he left to fetch a bucket - we pushed onward through and into the tumult, dodging horse bodies - Gentry ran up with a bucket and quickly sponged our five horses as we walked - we stopped somewhere near the in-gate to the pulsing area - take saddles off? no! - where did my other riders go? - "yes, saddles off!" yelled volunteer Dublin, directing traffic into the ring - we hesitated, not sure what to do first - I finally got my saddle off and just dropped it on the ground for lack of any better idea - "boots off too!" - Quinn wouldn't hold still because the others were - somewhere - Bruce grabbed him - I got the boots off and we moved into the pulse ring... I'd never been in such bedlam at a vet check. It was exhausting!

I hoped Quinn's pulse was down, because we weren't riding with heart rate monitors or stethoscopes, but by the time Quinn's pulse was taken by a volunteer while in line, he was down to 56 (criteria was 60). What a relief!

We'd lost some time in that mayhem just getting into the vet area, and though we now had an in time of 11:27 - from which our hour hold began, as long as we passed the vet check - we had to stand in a long vet line. Chris had offered me a cold Dr Pepper as soon as we walked in, but I had turned it down - BIG MISTAKE! - so I stood in the vet line, thirsty and hungry, hot, holding my horse for 20 long minutes. At least Quinn was chowing down on hay the volunteers kept handing me, but I was famished, and suddenly feeling very tired.

We finally got our turn with a veterinarian; I trotted Quinn out and he passed inspection - hooray! All five of our horses passed the vet check and were fit to continue on the Tevis trail! We left the vet ring following Nance and Jasbo, and wove our way through camp and other people and horses to get to the spot where our crew had set up our gear for us.

But no time for me to sit and rest: had to get the horses eating - they didn't want their grain, so Nance and I tried mixing something else - made sure they had plenty of hay because that's really all they wanted - worried about that a bit - ran to the portapotty which was clear back at the vetting area - ran back, must get myself a cold Dr Pepper, must grab something to eat - but couldn't sit and rest because I had to refill my water bottles, mix up one bottle with human electrolytes, grab a Gatorade, find my fanny pack to put two extra water bottles in - oh God, I must soak my Cool vest for the canyons! - but we didn't have enough water so I went to fetch another bucket but Bruce said he'd get it and I sat down for two minutes. Just two precious minutes. Just enough to make me realize how awfully weary I was already.

Bruce returned with the bucket of water and I jumped up to soak my vest, then I fetched another bucket of water for Quinn because he had not been drinking enough, then, crap, it was 20 minutes till our time out, and we better get saddled right back up, because we had an exit exam and the line of horses was already long for that.

Lunch was almost over already! I choked down the rest of my half a sandwich, saddled up Quinn, (my knee was fine, so I kept the sports saddle on), slipped on

Quinn's hackamore and put on my wet Cool vest and fanny pack, wet bandana and helmet - and off we went to the final vet line near the exit.

We all vetted through there again and had a few minutes to spare before our out time of 12:27 PM. I stood beside Quinn, keeping weight off him for a few more minutes, and just then realized that was the least restful hour vet check I'd ever experienced in my 12 years of riding endurance, and I also realized we'd all five successfully completed the first third of our journey towards Auburn.

But - no time to stop and reflect - have to keep pushing onward.

"Number 197, you're out!" Back in the saddle and back onto the trail to Auburn!

8: 2009 Tevis Cup - Phase II

The second "LD":

- Robinson Flat to Dusty Corners - 9 miles - Water stop
- Dusty Corners to Last Chance - 5 miles - Gate and Go
- Last Chance to Devil's Thumb - 4 miles - Water stop
- Devil's Thumb to Deadwood - 1 mile - Gate and Go
- Deadwood to Michigan Bluff - 7.5 miles - Water stop
- Michigan Bluff to Chicken Hawk - 1.5 miles - Gate and Go
- Chicken Hawk to Foresthill - 4 miles - 1 hour hold at 68 miles

The middle third of the Tevis trail: CANYONS and DUST... and HURRY. We weren't racing to win Tevis; we weren't racing the other competitors. We were racing the clock.

Through this section those cutoff times began to nag at us, eat away at our sense of comfort. I've never had to worry about cut-off times in rides, because I ride at a middle-of-the-pack steady pace, which easily gets me and my horse to the finish line. My theory has always been, "Trot when you can, walk when you have to." I thought this would apply to Tevis also, but Tevis required a serious re-evaluation of "have to."

I could add HEAT and CLIFFS here to this middle section too - stagnant, thick, humid heat (my opinion), and death-defying cliffs inches from my horse's hooves (a fact).

And don't forget the dust again. If it's true that Eskimos have 100 words for "snow," then Tevis riders should have 200 words for "dust." But if they do have those words, I haven't learned them yet, so dust, dust, dust. Permeating, god-awful, wretched dust.

All of this to deal with as the clock is inexorably ticking.

I was feeling pretty jazzed as we left Robinson. Tired, unrested and a little disconcerted from the chaotic vet check, but elated. I'd completed a third of the Tevis trail. At times, as we were zooming along, I still could not believe I was riding it! If Quinn had been pulled at Robinson, or earlier, I would have been very disappointed. Getting past Robinson had been my modest, unspeakable goal. I felt like I'd gotten my adventure's worth. Now, every vet check more that Quinn got under his girth was icing on the cake, and I'd be happy with however much further we got. The next big goal was Foresthill, eight or so hours from here.

We picked up a fast trot right out of Robinson, but slowed to a walk going down steep switchbacks through an old burn area. I noticed 13-year-old Chandler was squirming in her saddle. She had developed shin splints, and had vetwrapped them at the vet check, thinking that would help; but now they were seriously bothering her. We didn't stop moving, but Laura put El Din in front at a walk; and behind her, Chandler perched like a bird on a wire, first one leg then the other out of the stirrup and in front of her, as she peeled the wretched bandages off. (Did I say these were fairly steep switchbacks?) Then quickly her feet were back in her stirrups, and we were back at a fast trot, down and down the zig-zagging trail.

Chandler never complained, not about her shin splints or sore muscles or being afraid, or anything. She always said she was "Fine!" when I asked, and she always carried a big smile to accompany that.

Onto single track trails, logging roads, and cliff trails, we trotted, and trotted incessantly, and fast. I automatically switched diagonals with curves in the trail, almost always posting because it's hard to two-point in a sports saddle that keeps your legs so far in front of you. It was good for my knee though - so far it hadn't bothered me at all. I thought once, as Jasbo got a bit of a lead on us, that I'd urge Quinn to a canter for a while, so we could both use some different leg and back muscles, and Quinn responded by opening up another two gears at a trot, like a Standardbred in a sulky race.

"Canter!" my legs asked him again, and he upped the trot yet another gear, and we almost ran into Jasbo's butt! After that, I let Quinn decide what he wanted to do - he knew what he was doing without suggestions from me.

But there were the stumbles to deal with. He'd thrown in a few during the day - he was a "daisy clipper," didn't pick his feet up as he moved down the trail. It made for efficient trotting, but sure threw in some disconcerting trips on these ever-rocky trails. One was so hard it slammed my lower abdomen into the saddle pommel, enough to make me gasp and curse out loud. I found myself missing much of my surroundings for watching the trail - and I got to where at times I could feel the split second before a stumble was coming, and I was there to pick Quinn's head up before it went down too far. Every time he did it, I'd half yell at him, half pray: "ARGHHH! This isn't helpful for a finish at Auburn!"

Somewhere ahead was Dusty Corners and Last Chance. Kara, in the lead, had pulled out the card with the cutoff times and realized we were not even a half-hour ahead of schedule anymore. (She had to be kidding!) "Guys, we have to get moving! (I thought we were!) If I can average 10 miles per hour, we'll get there with 45 minutes to spare..." and with that, all we saw was a line of dust from Kara and Jack on the narrow trail etched into the side of the mountain.

Not that there wasn't dust everywhere, all the time. I was still breathing through my bandana when it got thick, but it was starting to sandblast my eyes. Boy, was I glad I'd cleverly packed my eyedrops for Foresthill, still several hours down the trail.

Dust, and more thick dust. We came up onto crossroads that had water troughs and a cloud of dust - our horses drank a bit and then we were quickly zooming back down the dusty trails. "That must have been Dusty Corners," Laura called over her shoulder. "Why'd they pick THIS spot to call Dusty Corners? It's ALL dusty!"

I began to become obsessed with the ubiquitous dust nuisance. I imagined it permeating my skin and starting to slow my blood flow. I wondered if the alveoli in my lungs were turning to mud rivulets. The song Dust in the Wind started ear-worming in my brain. As a writer, I tried to think of other words for dust: dirt infused? Soil laden air? I wondered how the Bedouins dealt with it, I wondered how the Dust Bowl people survived. Perhaps my brain was being infused and this dust obsession was the beginnings of delirium.

Kara kept up the fast pace, I kept my eyes on the narrow trail, and realized that I really hadn't been taking in much of the scenery. All this beautiful Sierra Nevada terrain, "THE MOST BEAUTIFUL RIDE EVER!" my uncle Dick had said, and most of what I had seen so far was 40 miles of trail and rock underfoot, ever watchful of where my horse might stumble next.

I lifted my gaze and saw, to my right, an awesome ridge of mountains far across the way and - gasp! - a wide, fathomless canyon pit below my stirrup stretching between me and that scenic ridge. I evaluated that 30-degree bare slope, with nothing for 500 feet down, then a forest hiding another 500 feet or so of slope down to the bottom, which I could not see.

Okay, *forget that!* and go back to watching where my horse is putting his feet on this two-foot-wide-trail-with-nowhere-to-go-but-forward-or-over-the-abyss, and be sure he avoids that big round stone, or that slickrock coming up that slants toward the edge of nothingness! I fleetingly wondered if this was maybe the infamous "Pucker Point," or the spot in the trail where a friend Lucy said gave her the heebie-jeebies; but I was glad I hadn't insisted **on the** details. If I'd had sense, I might have been a little scared here - this really was one of those wrong-step-and-you-die stretches of trail - but there was nothing to do but fly along. Which we did. Besides, walking wouldn't have made it better - we'd have just spent more time riding along the cliffs!

We arrived at Last Chance vet check 33 minutes ahead of the cut-off. It was rather mind-blowing - I didn't see how we could have been going much faster. And yet the leaders were probably hours ahead of us already. In fact, Melissa Ribley, who finished second, was two hours and ten minutes ahead of us at this check.

For once, there wasn't a big cluster of horses with us at the vet check. Quinn drank deeply - MUCH to my relief, and we stood in the shade while in the vet line. The horses chowed down on hay, and one volunteer sponged Quinn down. "Do me too!" I said.

"Really?"

"Yes!" The hot canyons were coming up next. He squeezed a sponge full of water down my neck and back, a blessed cool refresher for my Cool vest. We moved up to see the vet, and as the vet listened to Quinn's heart rate, he mumbled something before moving back on him to palpate his butt muscles and listen to his gut.

"What!?" I asked anxiously. What was wrong with Quinn?

The vet turned to look at me. "44."

"44!" That was Quinn's heart rate - a very low count for all the effort he'd put forth.

I was floored. "Wow!" The vet checked everything else - all good - and the vet scribe handed me back my vet card.

The vet said, "Wait!" The scribe grabbed the card back. Uh oh! The vet was listening to Quinn's heart again. Maybe he'd heard something - a murmur, or... oh no, what if something was really wrong! I held my breath.

The vet looked up at me and grinned. "Yep, 44. I just had to make sure I was hearing right."

That about put me over the moon. It was a pivotal point for me: I wouldn't be worrying about Quinn's pulse rate anymore. We were exactly halfway done with the ride, (halfway done!); despite the cracking pace it seemed we were going, my horse was pulling harder on me now than he had been this morning, with a heart rate of 44 here; and Nance had said, "Quinn will perk up after sunset." Well - he hadn't ever un-perked! Quinn had plenty of gas left in his tank.

Next: down into the first fabled canyon. This was the canyon where a friend Clydea had told me it was 114 degrees at the bottom one year she did Tevis. I wished I hadn't asked her. I was not looking forward to that! The five of us followed the trail down, switchbacking down, down into the heat, further down, steeper down, forever down.

Nance and I got off our horses and led them. We had ended up again in a long line of people and horses, in front of and behind us. You had to pay attention to the footing - very rocky, steep, tricky steps, big steps. A fall at this point would hold up the long line stretching behind us.

Had to just keep moving. It was terribly dusty. Hard to breathe, cloyingly hot (for me), no breeze (this side was in the sun), this was not fun, I didn't really want to be here, dust so thick and painful I had tears pouring down my face, but I didn't dare close my eyes for a brief respite. You had to keep moving, watching so your horse wouldn't jump on you at some of those big, precarious steps, down and down, quad muscles getting shaky, 1726 feet and almost two miles of down. The guy behind me had been off and running a lot of the Tevis trail - something like 17 miles already. We asked him if he had done the Western States 100-mile run on foot - over this same trail - a month before. "No, and after this, I don't want to!"

Zig-zagging forever downward, impossibly down, concentrating on the trail, too hot and dusty to converse or do anything else but gasp and cough and squint. The forest was punctuated with the plopping of hooves in dust, and the occasional clang when a steel shoe slipped on a rock.

And then, finally, the temperature dropped slightly and a new sound crept up toward us... water! We were getting close to the North fork of the Middle fork of the American River, the bottom of this forever-canyon – yahoo!

There was a small crowd of horses down off the trail going into the river to drink, and a little line of horses waiting to cross the Swinging Bridge over the river, a suspension bridge half a horse wide, 30 feet long. The sign said no more than three horses at a time. Nance had said if you got two horses on there the bridge would start to swing - no thanks! She waited till the horse in front of her had crossed.

Quinn and I followed when she was almost across. As we neared the end, the bridge started to sway a bit; Quinn was unbothered, and we just kept walking, and made it onto solid ground on the other side.

Then, after our horses took a quick drink, no time to reflect - mount right back up and keep right on going. What trail goes down must come back up - 1565 feet out of the canyon. This side was several degrees cooler since it wasn't in the sun - but just as steep. Steeper in some places. Quinn was panting like a dog as we switchbacked, climbing higher and higher, dirt and sweat coating him from ear tips to hooves, dripping sweat, straining muscles, pushing hard with the hind end, digging in and pulling himself up with his front end, step after hard-fought upward step, me leaning forward in my saddle, willing him the help he needed. I worried about it... what if this was too much, should I stop him and make him rest? What if his heart just beats so fast it quits and he keels over? If I stop him, would it be too hard to get going again? You don't want to stagger sideways on this trail because sideways is a drop-off. Is Quinn smart enough to stop himself if he needs a breather?

And one time he did stop on his own and pause... one, two, three, four, five seconds, his panting and slamming heart in synchronized pounding - and that was it; he pushed onward and upward. That was the only time all day and all night my amazing gray horse ever stopped to catch his breath - those five seconds climbing up that steep hot American River canyon.

We were back in a line of horses, putting one foot in front of the other up the trail. Nothing to do but keep moving. One guy's paint horse in front of us had stopped. He wouldn't move. Needed a breather. It fortuitously happened on a switchback corner where there was a tiny bit of extra room, and he was able to pull over, and several of us rode past without slowing, our line of horses straining upward past him, noses to tails. The guy got off to lead his horse.

The trail made a bend around a steep ravine... something caught my eye to the steep downhill side that was odd. I glanced over my left shoulder and saw something brown and white at the bottom. Not right... *not right*. That was a horse, and it should not be there - *could not* be there. Holy S***.

I looked again, at the brown and white body laying down in the green undergrowth, the head turned oddly, and it was not moving. We all saw it at the same time, and realized what it was. Gasps and sobs came from our line of riders.

I didn't dare look - was it wrong to stare? - but I couldn't help looking back. Big mistake. I saw a man, sitting on his dead horse, cutting something - bridle, lock of mane, I didn't know what it was, then looking upward to the heavens. The hand of finality grabbed at my throat and choked off my air. Some man just lost his horse, his partner, his friend.

One bad step, a freak instant where it all goes wrong. Sometimes you find that rock with your horse's name on it that makes him lame; sometimes you find a bad step with your horse's name on it - or your name - where it's all over. It was over for them.

There was no place to pull over to help - though there was nothing to rescue - and the line just kept slogging upward, onward - and for God's sake, keep paying attention to the trail, because this could happen to any one of us. It *had* happened to one of us. The strained silence, the tear-streaked black faces from our line of riders were a pitiful tribute to the shocking loss we just passed.

The steep climb went on. We all carried on and up, thinking, as our horses' panting filled the silence. Several volunteers who were hiking down to the dead horse and his rider pulled off the trail to let us march past, hanging onto trees so as not to slip down. "It's alright. We're going to help him," they said. They had a long hike down.

We finally spilled out at the top of the canyon at Devil's Thumb. Quinn was drenched in sweat, and I jumped off to sponge him and Jasbo (and myself) as they dove into a water tub for a drink. We didn't have much to say. We mounted up and kept moving the last mile to Deadwood vet check.

We were about 40 minutes before cut-off - and in a frustrating cluster of horses again. Our horses were starved and dove into the hay near the water troughs. By the time Nance and I got in line to vet our horses, it was a long one. We held hay for the horses to eat as we waited, and volunteers ran to fill our water bottles and hand us slices of watermelon to eat. We finally got to the vets, trotted out and back; our horses passed with flying colors, and we pulled over to wait for Kara, Laura, and Chandler in the chaos. Kara was held back by the vets (!) and told to go back and let her horse eat a while, because either his CRI was a bit high, or his gut sounds were low. What!? We didn't have time for this!

We didn't see Laura and Chandler in the maelstrom anywhere. Had they left already? Jack was eating with Kara, over by the water troughs again, there was still a long vet line that Kara and Jack weren't in, and the clock was ticking.

That old Cut-Off Time: haunting us, pressing us, stalking us, taking away from some of the fun of the ride. How long were we going to be here? Should we wait? Do we have to wait? Are we obligated to stick together? Was it selfish to want to leave Kara behind, after we'd all travelled 55 miles of hard trail together, our horses buddied up well? Do I ride my ride, or do I ride someone else's ride? And anyway I was riding Nance's horse, so it wasn't even completely my choice. Where were Laura and Chandler - back on the trail already? Is it all about having fun and experiencing this Tevis ride together, or is it about me myself, and finishing my Tevis ride myself? I had pictured Nance getting pulled, and me having to go on without her (yikes!). I'd pictured me getting pulled, and Nance going on without me. I hadn't planned on Kara or Laura or Chandler getting pulled, even when, before the ride, Chandler had asked all of us if we'd be her sponsor if her mom got pulled.

I looked at my watch for the thousandth time today, and said to Nance, "We *have* to go, we can't wait!" We'd now lost about 30 minutes here (at least our horses had been resting and eating all of that time), and if we kept up our same pace, we'd now be only 10 minutes ahead of cut-off times. ARGH!

Nance was on the fence. I knew she didn't want to abandon Kara, but... bottom line was, that clock was ticking. I held Jasbo and Quinn while she went to talk to Kara. Nance came back and said, "Let's go." I looked at my watch once more and didn't ask questions. The two of us mounted up and trotted away.

I don't remember the next seven and a half miles of the trail to Michigan Bluff - into the next canyon, and 2665 feet of descent into El Dorado canyon, and then climbing the other side - and I don't remember the trail, though I know Nance and I were rushing along it, and it was rocky, and it was dusty. Probably a combination of tiredness, hunger, time worries and a dead horse to think about. And heck, I probably couldn't see anything anyway because of the dust! My aching, scratched eyes were starting to give me a headache.

This Last Chance-to-Michigan Bluff trail was built in 1850, and used to be a maintained toll trail. Long trains of pack mules negotiated the steep, twisting trails to outfit the miners with supplies and carry the mined gold back out. Our horses' feet were following the footsteps of over a hundred years of mining history. The trails were steep and rocky and treacherous back then, and they weren't much different now.

I do remember popping out on the top of the canyon at Michigan Bluff. Once a tent city in the 1840's with the discovery of gold, then a permanent mining settlement, now it's a small ghost town. The city had to be moved from its canyon precipice in 1859, as mining activities threatened to erode the town off the cliff. $100,000 worth of gold per month was shipped out from the mines at Michigan Bluff during its heyday.

A few dozen people still lived here, and many of them were out enjoying the horse race passing through. They were out in the streets and sitting in chairs on their lawns, waving and cheering us on, still rooting for the back-of-the-pack riders. Quinn avoided the water troughs and trotted on down the road as if he were in a parade... onward for the mile and a half to the next gate and go vet check at Chicken Hawk; onward against the clock.

After a mile and a half of nice soft (dusty) logging road, Nance and I caught up with two smudged yellow shirts ahead of us - Laura and Chandler. The road dropped us into Chickenhawk vet check at around 30 minutes before cut-off time, and we had a nice surprise, our friends Jackie and Gretchen who were there to help us crew. They hopped in to sponge our horses, while volunteers jumped in to ply us with food ("What can I get you?") and fill our water bottles and take our horses' pulses.

By now, I'd finally figured it out: get into a vet check, immediately water your horse and sponge him down with cool water, grab some hay while you move on, go straight to the pulse takers, and if you're down, go straight to the vet. If you linger anywhere, you lose time, especially if there's a crowd of horses. Our horses could rest and eat briefly *after* they got through the vet inspection. It was a little late in the day to get that important sequence figured out, but something to practice the rest of the night.

It also helped that there weren't many horses here - we'd landed in a bubble between lines of riders. Quinn took about three minutes to pulse down - he was quite hot to the touch, and it was warm and muggy here, but we kept slowly moving closer to the vets, and as soon as he hit the criteria of 64, we vetted through. Jackie and Gretchen held our horses at piles of hay while we used the portapotties, and then grabbed one more slice of watermelon to eat before we mounted back up. I don't like watermelon, but I must have eaten half of a whole watermelon throughout the day. It was delicious today. I ate the pulp; Quinn finished the rinds.

The day had flown by, we had zoomed over the trails, and now, unbelievably - we were four miles from the hour vet check at Foresthill.

TEVIS CUP MAGIC

Foresthill! Clean clothes, food, EYEDROPS, Dr Pepper, a face wash (I hadn't washed my face till now, because the dirt was a good extra protective layer against the sun), a little rest (oh, PLEASE, let me be able to rest, just a little) - and, best of all, if we passed the vet check, two-thirds of the ride completed!

The last half mile into Foresthill is an uphill climb on a paved road. We dropped off the trail onto the road, and there were a few people clapping for us as we rode by. As we continued up the road, there were more people. Many were crew members waiting for their horses, and others were just observers, people out to take in the spectacle, to cheer the riders and horses on. Crew members cheered for any and every horse and ride that went by. I was very amused at the people who were very amused and pointing at my blackened face and once-yellow-now-black shirt. They cheered, "Good job!" which made me feel pretty good - me, a back of the pack rider - and added a bit more straightness to my seat on my horse, and a bit more spring in my step when I got off to lead him in - much more energy than I felt a half hour ago.

As we got closer to the in-time gate, and the crowd grew, and the cheers increased, I started to feel pretty darn great. Friends' faces were popping out of the crowd, calling my name. "Hey Merri - I'm so glad you're riding!" "Great job!" "You go girl!" We got more cheers, I started to get hugs. A friend Sue, crewing for someone else, jumped in to unsaddle my horse. A little girl with a water hose jumped in to spray off Quinn and Jasbo. Dick and Carolyn were there by the number takers and hugged me, even though I rubbed half my dust and mud off on them. Another surprise, a friend Mickie was there, and she followed us to help at our crew spot.

We moved into the vetting area, got our horses' pulses taken (they were already below the 64 criteria) and we moved straight on to the vet, holding hay for our famished horses to eat while we waited in line. Bruce offered to trot Quinn out for me. I said - surprised that I wasn't hurting at all - "I think I can do it!" And I did. Quinn looked just terrific, alert and not tired, as he stood in the twilight for the vet who took his pulse. When we turned to trot out down the sandy lane and back, we both jogged as if we were vetting in on Friday, light and easy. The vet finished his check and smiled at me: "Good job!" Those are the most wonderful words you can hear when you've officially passed the vet check at Foresthill!

Nance had finished her trot out with Jasbo, (the two horses neighed and turned their heads as we trotted past each other) and we high-fived each other as we left the ring together. We had finished two-thirds of the Tevis trail - 68 miles down, only 32 more miles to go! It hardly seemed possible that I - who five days before had no idea I'd be here - really had a chance to finish my first Tevis ride! What an awesome horse I was riding!

Following Bruce to the crewing area that he and Chris and Gentry had set up for us, I passed Julie Suhr on the way. She gave me a big hug, and when she said, "See you at the finish," I choked up and I couldn't answer. She said it matter-of-factly, and, coming from Julie, a finish really did seem logical.

First thing I did, once Quinn was set up with grain and hay (I was somewhat dismayed he and Jasbo still weren't much interested in their grain, though at least they were devouring hay), was a CHANGE OF CLOTHES! I was wet from head to toe - from sweat, and my Cool vest - so I pulled out a new set of clothes, ran between the trees, and peeled everything off. Wow! A clean and dry set of clothes - even though I was still dirty - gave me a whole new perspective on life. Then I washed my face. WOW! Now I could face another eight hours of riding! One more thing: EYEDROPS!

I reached into the crew bag - I couldn't find the eyedrops. *Uh oh.* I dug through my emergency kit in my saddle bag - no eyedrops. I frantically dug through crew bags and again in my saddlebags - the eyedrops were *missing*. I asked my crew, and I asked all the people around me, but nobody had eyedrops. Oh dear, my eyes were already killing me, and this was going to haunt me down the trail, I just knew.

But nothing to do about it, because I must keep moving: must eat something, fill water bottles, fetch more horse water because Jasbo just knocked his bucket over, sit a few minutes, (oooh, maybe that wasn't a good idea after all, because now I realized how really tired I was becoming), find some peanut butter crackers to stuff in my pocket for the ride to the next vet stop, find a headlamp and duct-tape that on my helmet for the coming darkness, worry a little about Quinn because he looked like he had to pee, but I swear he hadn't peed at all today. I scattered some hay underneath him, because horses don't like to pee on hard ground, and they love to pee on hay... but he wouldn't go. I dumped my fanny pack with the two extra bottles of water, because I figured I'd come across plenty more water at the vet checks on the way; and anyway I'd be carrying three bottles on my saddle.

Kara and Jack arrived into Foresthill in good shape, about 20 minutes behind us. Gretchen and Jackie showed up at our crew spot to help. Along with Mickie, they helped tape glowsticks to our horses' breast collars. I really, really longed to lay down, just for a minute or two... but I knew that wasn't a good idea.

Time to resaddle anyway. We needed to leave on time, because still we were only 40 minutes ahead of cut-off - the time clock was ever ticking right behind us. Equipment on and everything ready, I started leading Quinn after Nance and Bruce and Jasbo across the parking lot to the out-timer. Laura and Chandler had already gone; they were a few minutes ahead of us. Suddenly Quinn pulled me to a stop. What - unwilling to go on? He had never once shown any sign of reluctance all day. I asked him again, but he wouldn't move... then I realized he'd stopped over a pile of hay - and he started to pee! And the color looked good - a light hydrated yellow - a relief! I cheered out loud - endurance riders tend to get a little excited about their horse's good-colored pee. Now Quinn followed me at a trot to catch up with Nance and Jasbo.

I was just about to climb on my horse's back, as Nance was doing, then, "Crud! I forgot my chaps!" I have to ride with half chaps, or my legs get rubbed, or pinched by the stirrup straps. I couldn't stand that for eight more hours. Argh! I threw Quinn's reins at Bruce, and ran (argh!) back across the parking lot to our crew spot - and I couldn't find my chaps. Gentry brought his flashlight over to help me look - it was now dark - and we finally found them. I raced back across the parking lot with my chaps in hand - now out of breath and hot - and found Bruce and Nance and the horses. I sat in the dirt in the spotlight by the out-timer and fumbled to get my chaps on. I finally got them zipped up, mounted up on Quinn, and we were out, only a minute behind our out-time.

Nance and I headed out, onto our last third of the Tevis trail, the California loop. A volunteer stopped traffic for us as we crossed the road and headed out into the darkness.

Eight hours or so ahead lay our destination: Auburn and the finish line.

9: 2009 Tevis Cup - Phase III

The final "LD":

- Foresthill to Francisco's - 17 miles - Gate and Go
- Francisco's to River Crossing - 3.3 miles - No check
- River Crossing to Lower Quarry - 6 miles - Gate and Go
- Lower Quarry to No Hands Bridge - 2 miles - No Check
- No Hands Bridge to the Finish - 4 miles - Finish vet check

The last third of Tevis: CLIFFS and DUST. A few more words come to mind and blur together: Blackness, Hurtling, Insane, Enough Already, Disconnected, Fatigue, Intrigue, Thirst, Bliss, Misery, and (deserves mentioning again) Dust.

We left the Foresthill vet check in the dark, at 8:52 PM. Refreshed, starting over, only eight more hours or so of riding to go - I felt we could actually do this! Quinn led the way onto the streets of Foresthill, under the streetlights, past honking cars, past bars and outdoor cafes with partying people who cheered us on our way. A man on a street corner holding his little boy on his shoulders said, "See those horses? Those aren't just endurance horses, those are *Tevis* horses!" Made me feel pretty darn special. I was riding Quinn, a TEVIS horse. Quinn was a special horse, and I was his lucky partner on this day and night.

We followed a few riders off the streets, onto the trail that is the start of the legendary California loop with its miles and miles of cliff riding - as opposed to all the earlier miles and miles of cliff riding. We could see the lights of Auburn on the horizon, across the canyon of the American River, 16 miles away as the raven flies, 32 miles by challenging trail. The almost-full moon was a tiny spotlight reflection on the river far below, and it lit up the wide trail before us.

I reached down for assurance that the Raven and the Tevis guardian angel were safely ensconced in the Raven bag. This Raven would be taking the long way to Auburn with me.

Nance and I had fallen in with Ernie on his paint horse Captain Calypso, and Cassandra, riding Imasweetsteele. We trotted along the trail together, telling stories, slowly starting to chip away at the miles. Quinn had never flagged all day, and now he was pulling on the reins even harder. I'd even had to put my gloves back on. Absolutely incredible.

And now is when I knew for certain that I would finish the Tevis with a sound horse. IF, of course, Quinn didn't trip and fall, IF he didn't hit that rock with his name on it, IF we didn't fall off a cliff, IF we made it to Auburn in time, by 5:15 AM, I would complete Tevis with a solid, strong, sound horse. A lot of IF's in there, but I knew Quinn wouldn't just go lame or metabolically quit before we finished. It felt phenomenal and astonishing, to be on a horse that felt so unbelievably strong after 17 hours on the trail.

We eventually became a line of riders again - too dark to see how many; we hard more than saw them - when the trail started down into the forest, down switchbacks into the black hole of the American River canyon. With the single track downward came the thick dust churned up by hooves in front of and below us. The trail was quite steep (and I found out later *how* steep, something I was glad I didn't know), and even in the blackness you could sense this was a trail you didn't want to screw around on. It was very dusty - hard to breathe, and, unbelievably, I'd forgotten my breathing bandana. At times I'd try holding my shirt over my mouth, but this was a rugged trail and I had to keep both hands on the reins. I gave up and just choked down the dust. The red headlight on my helmet would often illuminate a thick red cloud around my head and I could make out nothing else. Sometimes I'd shut the light off and just hang on in the dark. Sometimes I'd shut my eyes the dust was so bad. It was starting to *really* aggravate my eyes.

Back and forth, Quinn would make the sharp switchback turns, forever going downward in a line of riders. A couple of times I turned on my light and looked down at the turn - eek! He stepped way too close to the outside drop-off on that one and I corrected him! Was he doing this EVERY TIME?

Better, I think, that I not watch and try to control what he was doing, and just let him pick his own way. He *did* know what he was doing... didn't he? Horses could see well in the dark... *couldn't* they? No point in worrying about it - sometimes you just have to trust your horse. There was no room, no time to be scared. Nothing you could do anyway but keep moving with the line of horses. If anybody stopped, there would be trouble.

In the pitch dark as we descended, sometimes all I could see was a line of dim floating green lights - most breast collars had three glowsticks taped to them - and they levitated eerily toward us, above and below us on the switchbacks. At times, Quinn would watch them, swiveling his head, fascinated, as he walked along - AHH! I'd squirm in my saddle silently. Please, Quinn, turn your head back to the trail! Don't trip or fall off here for watching the other horses! Sometimes all I'd see in the blackness were sparks kicked up by horseshoes striking rocks.

When we came to very tricky spots in the trail where the lead horse slowed to cross - a little spring over wet rocks, or a pile of rocks, or a branch at about human head level requiring you to duck over your horse's neck - we'd pass the information to the rider behind us - you could hear it going back down the line in the dark: "Rocks!" "Watch it here!" "Headache!"

Nance and Jasbo were in front of a few horses in the lead for a while, trying to feel their way in the dark. The red light on her helmet helped, but it only just penetrated the blackness. Some horses are sensible enough to slow down over rocks, and trot when it gets better. Jasbo would trot over anything, so Nance was just guessing when it was safest to trot.

I'd been talking to the guy behind me for a while before I realized it was Bruce and his Tennessee Walker, John Henry. I glanced back, noticed his hat, and the glow of his clean white shirt (still clean! Surely he changed to a new one at Foresthill!). He offered to go in front, because he knew the trail, and his horse had a great energetic walk, and was very sure-footed. Bruce took over, and became our Trail Master of the Dark for a while; John Henry kept up a good confident pace for all of us.

I kept waiting for that first little water stop/trot-by, whatever it was, coming up fairly soon. I'd checked my vet card twice upon leaving Foresthill; the stop/vet check was four miles out of Foresthill. I was going to fill my water bottles, because I'd already used half of my supply - some to douse my head, which was uncomfortably hot under my helmet, and some to wash down the dry peanut butter crackers I'd brought along and was trying to choke down. Maybe I could rinse my eyes out too, because they were killing me.

The trail kept going, and going - *surely* we'd gone four

miles by now - and Bruce kept talking about the vet check at Francisco's which was 17 miles from Foresthill. It took me a while - like hours - to comprehend that there WAS no water stop/vet check before Francisco's. We were ON the long 17 mile loop to Francisco's, which was the next vet check. There was *no* drinking water to be had between now and then.

I pulled out my card and turned on my headlamp and looked once more, and I could scarcely believe my scratched eyeballs. Maybe because of them I could no longer read. Indeed there was no stop before Francisco's listed on there. Whattheheck! Could I have become delirious? Was this a dust induced delirium?

That was a crushing blow. Now that I had a couple more hours of slow miles to go till I could get more water, I started obsessing over it. I needed water - I was terribly hot, lightheaded, my head felt like a sauna, I was dreadfully hungry (but couldn't eat because I didn't have water to wash any dry crackers down), seriously thirsty (but now I had to ration my remaining water), my eyes were hurting horribly from the dust, this was one Long-A** ride, and whose bloody idea was this, anyway. Both the trail and my thoughts were dark.

That trail to Francisco's was the longest stretch of miles on an endurance ride ever. *Ever.* On and on it went. And though it felt that the clock ticked by slowly, the ride time still ticked mercilessly on, and we could not let up. And still the rocky trail and tricky footing was unforgiving. It never eased. We flew through the dark, trotting on, a stumble here, sparks from hooves flying there, on and on, and on forever.

I found myself zoning out when I trotted, the pace unchanging for so long in the dark with no solid visual reference to anything around me. I wasn't really riding; I wasn't really on a horse. I was somewhere off to the side (to the right side, to be exact), in the ether as we flew down the trail, and a few times I had to physically shake myself to get me to come back into myself and on my horse, to hold onto those reins and pay attention, be ready for a stumble, or a duck to the left or right on the trail.

For we seemed to be going impossibly fast in the black void. A wild roller coaster in the darkness - flat ground (with rocks, of course), up, flat, down, up (oof! my stomach got jammed), zip left, zip right, horse stumbles, pick his head up, zip right, up, left, down. Sometimes I leaned left for an imagined (hallucinated?) turn, but Quinn went right. So much dust the red light from my helmet just showed a thick red cloud of what was going into my eyes and down my desperately dry and parched throat and into my lungs - better to shut it off and be in the dark and stay very centered on my horse to follow whichever way he zipped with the trail that I couldn't see.

I'd find myself disconnecting again... I wasn't particularly hallucinating, I wasn't hearing voices, but I was seeing a few extra things... lights... green lights... bright green outlines of things... (that weren't there)... just... *things*... before I'd pull myself back to the present. Was it really 20 hours ago I climbed on this horse, 75 miles from here? Or was that another century, or a thousand miles away I did that, or was that another human being that did it? And did it really matter?

For some long stretches we were on a narrow trail above the American River - far, *far* above the American River - straight down below. Ah, so these were the cliffs I'd heard (but purposely not read) about, on this California loop. I was glad I hadn't known about these cliffs, or they might have worried me. Though the moon was hidden behind one of the walls of the canyon, the sky was bright enough to illuminate the drop-off of the white cliffs below my left stirrup. One star was a bright beacon reflected in the water. It was hard to gauge exactly how far the river was at the bottom - 500 feet? A thousand? But one thing for sure was, if you went over the edge, there was nothing to stop you reaching that river. You might bounce once...

but you might not.

If I had any sense, this is where I'd be scared... but I really was too tired to care, and nothing to do anyway, but keep moving over this rocky trail, to eat up those miles as that lurking clock kept ticking down.

Sometimes we'd go through a little strip of trees, then we'd pop back out on the cliff trail. Rarely we'd end up on a logging road for a bit, a lovely change, and we'd really let fly, though we couldn't really see anything more here; it was all still blackness. It was easier to stay focused and in the present here because of the pine tree branches that would suddenly appear in my red light at the last second and slap me in the face. Luckily they were polite, small branches. Most of them. One ripped Nance's headlamp off her helmet... but no time to stop, go back and look for it - we just kept trotting down the trail.

Then, in the dark, flying at a trot, it happens, the thing I'd been dreading: The Big Stumble. Not one stumble and recover, but a dramatic threeinarow - SLAM-SLAM-SLAM! *This is it,* flashes in my head, *we're going down.* A picture rushes through my brain: Quinn plows into the ground, flips over, I'm underneath.

I instinctively brace my feet in the stirrups and hands on the reins as it happens, so fast. The fourth stride Quinn catches himself - or I catch his head - from going all the way down (at the next vet check, I find a cut on his nose where it hit the ground) and he leaps forward into another trot gear - almost as if embarrassed at the stumble and now he has to catch up quickly.

Now I have adrenaline shooting throughout my body and out my fingertips into the night; now I'm very awake and aware that we almost lost it there, and that hurtling through the darkness like this where I can't see anything is sheer insanity... but there is nothing to do but keep careening forward, because the time clock is ticking, always ticking, relentlessly counting down our time left to the finish. I'm not quite scared now, just very aware, very alert. My hallucinations evaporate in a poof. We are a looooooong way from help if anything happens. Somewhere in here is where, in 2007, Nance passed a place in the trail where someone was waiting at the edge, with a man and horse who'd fallen over the cliff and was awaiting evacuation. And besides, there is no time for an accident, because it would waste time, and we have no time to waste! Must keep going, must keep pushing.

And my horse is going. Quinn is pulling even harder on me. If I let up on the reins at all, he's right on Jasbo's butt. We're back to the discussion we had with each other at the beginning of the ride, 80 miles earlier. Do I hold him back more as he pulls harder, so he can see where he's putting his feet, or trust him and let him go as fast and as close to Jasbo as he wants, risk clipping heels?

It's midnight: my eyes are killing me, (I wonder - can I permanently damage my eyes with this much dust?), one more stumble like that and this horse is going to kill me, if he stumbles like that on this narrow cliff trail... well, don't even think about *that*, my head is very hot, I'm thirsty, fatigued, why am I doing this, I am ready for this ride to be over. And I NEED WATER. I feel like crap. Hurry up and get the end of the trail here, or pull me, I'm ready for this to be done one way or the other. I got my money's worth, enough already.

But I have at least four more hours in the saddle.

And then someone says, "Look, see the lights? That's Francisco's!" It is still a mile or two away, but the lights are like a magnet, drawing us in - this godawful long loop is over!

We jump off and walk down the road in to Francisco's, head straight to the pulse takers - our horses are below the 68 criteria, I grab precious cool water from a volunteer and down the entire bottle as we continue straight to the vets - pass with no problems - and take our horses back to the hay so they can eat. Time cut-offs be darned, the horses are hungry, and, "If I don't eat something, NOW, I'm going to die!"

Nance agrees, "Ohmigod so am I!"

<><><><><>

I looked over the pile of delicious treats baked by the volunteers. Oh, how I wished I could eat those desserts, but I couldn't, because I'd get nauseous while riding. I debated over sandwiches, and picked a peanut butter and honey that I split with Nance. I have never eaten peanut butter and honey, because I don't like it, and this sandwich went down so good and so fast, Nance and I split another as we collapsed on the ground by our chowing horses. We guzzled cold water and Gatorade, and volunteers filled our bottles for the trail.

Wow, we both felt SO much better - and now we had only 15 miles to go - *15 more miles to the finish!* We could do this!

Now a glance at our watches - 12:40 AM: recommended time-in here was 1 AM, cut-off 1:45 AM - time to mount up and get going! Just as we were about to climb aboard, Kara and Jack arrived - they'd caught up with us!

"I pushed Jack harder than I should have, but, well... I'm here," Kara said. She wanted to stay with us, so she went straight to the vets, vetted Jack through, gave him a few handfuls of hay, and without grabbing any food or drink for herself, she mounted up, and we took off down the trail.

Now, the ride was different. Now the end was in sight and in our grasp. Now, this was all we had left, and I memorized it: three miles, then six miles, then two miles, then four miles - and the Finish! That made it sound even easier than 15 miles!

"What's the first thing you're going to do when we get back?" Nance asked. Now that we were close, we could start thinking about it. "Sleep? Eat? Brush your teeth? Shower?"

All good choices, but - "EYEDROPS!" I shrieked. It felt like my dusty and scratched eyeballs were bleeding, but now they'd only have to do it for another couple of hours!

Onward in the dark three miles to the American River crossing - along more cliffs, trotting fast all the way - we'd picked up Cassandra again. Ernie's horse had been pulled at Francisco's. Cassandra got us all talking a bit, then Kara and Nance and I started singing songs from the Sound of Music: "Favorite Things" to take our mind off this looooooong tiring journey, and, of course, "Climb Every Mountain," because that's what we had done today! Though Julie Andrews would have been horrified because we sounded weak and out of tune with voices choked and scratchy with fatigue and dust, several people joined in and we gave it our best croaks. Kara made up a personalized verse having to do with the final Auburn mountain to climb and fording the American River.

We descended to the river, where our passage across was lined with glowsticks floating on lines strung across the water. Volunteers were down here - their tents set up to grab a snooze after the last riders passed - taking our numbers. Our horses plowed into the water. Cool and refreshing, it came to above my ankles. Jasbo and Quinn seemed to linger in it instead of going straight across.

Stepping out of the river, after a good shake off, and starting up the other side, we gave a whoop - now, just six miles, then two miles, then four miles left! The horses picked up a fast pace though the trail led uphill. Quinn knew where he was. Jasbo sensed the excitement. We zipped along, and the six miles to the Quarry - which took over an hour - disappeared under fast flying hooves. It all seemed to be happening more quickly now.

We pulled into the Lower Quarry - the last vet check

at 94 miles - at 3:31 AM. Cut-off time for arrival was 3:45 AM. We were just 14 minutes ahead of the clock - incomprehensible!

Volunteers threw blankets over our horses' butts as we arrived - it was a little cooler here (thank goodness! I was no longer feeling so heat-stroked). They offered us anything, "Food? Water? Hold your horse?" No, thanks, gotta keep moving! We vetted through, pulled our starving horses away from the hay - we didn't dare linger. We climbed aboard our marvelous horses one more time, and we were off into the darkness once more.

The countdown: two more miles to No Hands Bridge, then four more miles to the finish. Our horses got a bit confused leaving the Quarry: Kara took off first, I trotted after, and Jasbo was last... but he thought he was leaving Quinn behind. Big whinny, and he stopped. Nance couldn't get him to move. Louder whinny. Quinn, trotting up ahead, answered, turned himself around, and we flew back to Jasbo. Whinny-cry-snuffle *Oh there you are, I thought I left you! No I'm here! Nicker nicker.* We turned them back up the road and took off laughing and cantering after Kara.

We were helped across the highway out of Francisco's by volunteers. "Thank you guys for being here!" we hollered over our shoulders as our horses pulled us fast up the hill. The clock ticked, the two miles flew by, and we were crossing No Hands Bridge. It was wider than I thought, and had rails - no big deal. I guess there was a high drop to the river but I didn't notice - we were already across it, and moving onward.

ONLY FOUR MORE MILES TO THE FINISH!

I know we will probably make it. Keep flying along, it will be close, but we are almost there. We trot when we can, walk when we have to. Nance is in the lead, though she has no light and is going blindly. Should she gamble trotting over this stretch? Walk here? How's the time? Check my watch. Doesn't really matter anyway, because I have no idea how far we have to go. Cat and mouse game with the clock. Will we make it? Will we get there too late? It is suspenseful; it is exciting; it is *fun!* If we make it on time - *oh my God!* - there is a silver buckle at the end, handed to me by Julie Suhr... and if we don't make it on time, well, then we aren't meant to make it, and I don't get a buckle from Julie, and we don't get a completion, but my incredible horse has gone a hundred miles over these mountains anyway, and we have done it.

We catch up with a line of people. Now we can't go our own pace, but have to go at the pace of those in front of us. Now the factors vary more, and the exciting tension ticks up a notch. Will we make the finish in time? Will this line slow us down? Are we walking too much? If we trot here, will a horse slip and go down? If anything happens to anybody on this narrow trail, we will all be held up.

But I'm not worried, even though I don't know exactly how much more we have to go, because I'd seen the sweep riders at the Quarry, mounted up and preparing to leave. When Nance and Chris finished together in 2007 they'd been just ahead of the sweep riders, who'd said, "Don't worry, we'll get you there in time." If we are going too slow now, they'll catch up with us. No worries, or... *almost* no worries. Just exhilarating anticipation, exciting uncertainty. Whether or not we finish in time, there is nowhere else I want to be than right here right now.

And then: the damper on the whole final few miles. Someone has come up right behind me, someone in a terrible tizzy. "Guys, we have to move here. We have to trot! Ohmigod they aren't trotting ahead of us!" Surely she can see, or at least hear, that we can't move any faster, we are in a line of horses. Then comes the wailing: "We aren't going to make it! OHMIGOD! You have to TROT! PLEASE! OH MY GOD!!"

On the switchbacks above us, the leader must hear

TEVIS CUP MAGIC

the hysteria below him; but on the straight trail, I get all of it. Every anguished shriek. Miles of it. Totally ruins the atmosphere. Now I, who had been semi-relaxed and enjoying the hunt, am starting to get a little worried. What if we don't make it, what if we are overtime after we've come all this way, stuck behind a line of traffic, oh no! On and on the hysteria goes in my ears. I am ready to jump off my horse and whip out the duct tape to clamp over that hysterical voice in the dark.

Another line of riders comes up behind us, and one or two voices from there are in a frenzy also. "We need to move faster!"

At which point I am able to realize - so WHAT if we don't make it! It's all part of the Tevis luck. You spend too long at a vet check and you lose minutes. You lose a shoe, you lose minutes. You stop to help someone, you walk too long over a stretch, you get caught behind a wall of riders on a single track and you have to walk, you get behind a rider and horse that helps pull your weary butt and your tired horse along, you fall off a cliff, you get a clear stretch on your own, you are given a horse to ride five days before Tevis, you get to ride with four friends who are also probably going to make it to the finish, you find or miss that rock with your horse's name on it that lames him, you get stuck with a hysterical rider behind you - it's all part of the Tevis Luck that the indifferent Tevis Gods dole out at random with amusement, and sometimes it has nothing to do with you or your horse personally. The Tevis Gods enjoy applying different effects of fatigue in the wee hours of the morning to different riders: some hallucinate some pretty spectacular visions; some riders get sick in the dark and throw up; some become hysterical over things; some become irritated over things like hysterical people.

And I am at peace once again with the outcome - either we finish in time and I get a buckle, or we don't finish in time, and I don't get a buckle, (heck - I don't even wear belts!), but I have an incredible sound horse that has carried my dog-tired butt 100 miles on an absolutely amazing ride across the Sierra Nevada mountains to Auburn, in more or less 24 hours. It is all good.

Although I sure do wish I had earplugs.

Kara manages to slip around some riders ahead of us, and she is out of there. We can't blame her; she'd had enough of The Hysterical Rider too. Nance and I end up behind our fellow Idaho rider Max Merlich and his mule Junior. They'd tried the Tevis trail the previous year and gotten pulled. Now they are but a few miles from the finish line.

Now, everyone knows you can NOT get a mule to trot, if a mule does not want to trot, and Junior did not want to trot right then and there. But the verbal panic abuse blasting Nance and me is irritating Max enough that he risks life and limbs pulling over on a steep switchback to let a few of us go by. Nance and I have no room to pull over also to let anybody by us, so Nance flies along - in the pitch black, still leading the way, followed by me and Quinn, who are still stalked by the distraught rider.

We come to a wider spot in the trail. We pull over. "Go by - PLEASE!" I say, "GO!"

But The hysterical rider will not pass us. She'd rather weep and lament behind us. So we fly onward in the dark, on the twisting trail. We pop out at Robie Point at some welcomed water troughs. Jasbo and Quinn choose to stop and drink. The hysterical rider is almost sobbing, "We don't have time to drink! OHMIGOD!" as she lets her horse drink. The volunteer manning the water stop tries to soothe her: "You have plenty of time! Even if you walk in all the way from here, you'll make it!"

"Nooooo we won't! OHMIGOD!"

One or two riders trot past us up the trail. "JUST GO!" I say, gesturing down the open trail - "PLEASE! GO!" but the rider will not go!

Nerves taut now, the last final bit. Hysteria behind me, absolute irritation inside me: exasperation at overwrought riders who maybe should have left at least one of the vet checks all day just *five minutes sooner,* vexation that I'm bothered by it when all was so peaceful and exciting, aggravation that the Tevis Gods have planted a rider like this behind me to stretch and test my nerves this last part. The luck of the draw indeed!

One more small narrow spot in the trail to pass; Nance and I yank over to the side quickly, in desperation. A number of riders including The Hysterical Rider fly past us. Hallelujah!!

Now we rejoin the line; now it is back to trotting madly in the dark, back to the exciting hunt, silent but for electrified, fluttering nerves and trotting hooves over the dark, twisting single-track trail. We are wrestling it out with the Tevis Gods and the relentless time clock. I stop looking at my watch. The time doesn't matter anymore. My horse knows where we are. Quinn pulls and pulls on the reins, following Jasbo's butt. The dark goes on and on, but I recall someone saying that it goes on and on and suddenly you pop over the hill and you're done. Where are we in this on-and-on darkness with the clock running out?

A glow up ahead! A whoop from far ahead along the line of horses - hollers, whistles from the long line of riders working its way down to us - we take up the yelling and pass it on down the line because we know what it means - and all of a sudden we spill out over the top - the finish line under the lights at Auburn - and it is over.

OHMIGOD - we've arrived at Auburn!

I still haven't looked at my watch, but from the enthusiastic cheers of the awaiting crews and friends, I know we've made it in time. Nance and I are in the middle of a long line of riders - all 18 of us arriving at the same time, I find out later, at 4:56 AM. Plenty of time - 19 minutes! - to spare! 10 more riders arrive after us - two of them exactly at 5:15 AM cut-off, and one luckless man who is lost off trail the last few miles is overtime.

It is a whirlwind from here, and my brain suddenly

goes wobbly. I lose Nance, yell for her, follow her voice, push through the crush to get to her and Jasbo; we are rushed right away over the little bridge to the vet area; don't see any water for Quinn to drink, none to sponge him off with; hug some people; Quinn is starved, diving for dried grass as a volunteer comes to take his pulse; "68" - criteria is 68... maybe I should sponge him off before we go to the vet?... that's a little too close for comfort for me, what if his pulse goes up again as he walks to the veterinarian?

A veterinarian waves us over. It's a friend Ray Randall. He gives me a smile. I must look shell-shocked. He takes Quinn's pulse. "68." Whew! But yikes! Still too close for me. What if his CRI is high, when we trot back? "Trot out to cone three," Ray points. Ready Quinn? Our final trot-out of the day/night/morning, our final gait judgement of the ride.

We trot to cone three on the grass. I don't look, but I know, absolutely, that Quinn is sound behind me, and we have almost done it. We turn around. We start trotting back to the vet. I look up, and - *OH NO!* The vet is gesturing to another vet - "Come here quickly, watch this horse trot!" My heart plummets to the ground - Quinn is *LAME* and they are going to ask me to trot again, with two vets watching! *This can't be!*

Then I realize I am trotting toward the wrong vet, that Ray is over to my left. He is waving at me - "Yoohoo, this way," he calls laughing.

I say, "Oops!" as I zag back toward him. "You want me to trot out again?" But he isn't even watching the final steps of Quinn's trot out, because Quinn is sound as a dollar. Nance has already vetted through and completed with Jasbo, and even before Ray takes Quinn's pulse once more, we are hugging each other, with tears running down our faces.

Ray gives me the nod, and the congratulations - *OHMIGOD - WE JUST FINISHED THE TEVIS!*

TEVIS CUP MAGIC

I am suddenly whooped. I lurch after Nance's husband Bruce, who's leading us to the stadium, where we are now supposed to get back on our horses and ride their "victory lap" - poor horses just want to eat, they are grabbing at anybody who walks by with hay and yanking it out of their arms - and oh God, I just want to lie down. We climb on our horses once more, and trot the victory lap around the track together, the announcer not quite getting Nance's statistics right, and not even getting around to my name. There are only three people in the grandstand anyway at this ungodly time of morning, and one is my aunt Carolyn, who's waited up all night and morning, and is clapping and cheering me on, and she yells out my name - "Alright Merri! Way to go!" and we are all laughing as Jasbo and Nance and Quinn and I move out of the stadium. We jump off our horses and they grab mouthfuls of hay from Bruce, and we cheer for the other Bruce, who finished in our group at the same time, as he takes his victory lap, his first Tevis finish, on his big Tennessee Walker John Henry.

Laura and Chandler have finished eight minutes ahead of us, and Kara has finished in our big group. Three minutes behind us, Max Merlich and Junior finish - that makes the Idahoans six for six this Tevis.

But we aren't thinking of any of that. We stumble after Bruce to the horse trailer and pen that he'd set up for the horses in one of the parking lots. Quinn and Jasbo dive into their hay and grain. Nance and I can't quite figure out what to do next and how to do it, but we manage to think hard enough to put blankets on the horses and wrap their legs as the sky is starting to lighten - dawn over Auburn.

Stagger into the trailer and fall into bed. Find my eyedrops - *ohmigod* – *heaven.*

Can't remember if I took any clothes or shoes off or not. Pass out.

Finished Tevis.

OHMIGOD, I finished Tevis.

10: Tevis Epilogue

Now that the dust of Tevis has settled (pun!) I can sum it up in one word - if that's possible - Amazing. Well, maybe two words - Amazing, and Dust.

There is nothing easy about the Tevis Cup, not from the moment you start at 5:15 AM, until you finish - wherever that may be along the trail. Every endurance ride has its challenges and difficulties, but the Tevis Cup has 100 miles of it. It's extreme, challenging, relentless, frantic, exhilarating, heart-breaking, exhausting, exasperating, beautiful, insane, exciting, treacherous.

Yes, the Tevis trail is dangerous. However, though the Tevis has many (many) miles of perilous steep dropoffs and cliffs to ride along, many endurance rides have treacherous trails. You don't even have to have a dangerous trail to have a human or horse accident. You don't have to ride endurance to have a human or horse accident. Heck just being around horses can be dangerous. Anybody who owns a horse knows that even if he is just standing in a padded stall, he can find a way to kill himself, or you. As for humans, just walking out your front door can be dangerous. You can die sitting on your couch.

Everybody has to go some way, so you might as well

not fret about it, and do what you enjoy doing.

We choose to take our horses on endurance rides, and hopefully, they do get some enjoyment out of it. I know my horse did. We put their lives at risk riding them, asking them to do things... but any horse is at risk, be it the most pampered pet horse or a wild mustang. Every horse has to go some way too, so it may as well be something he enjoys doing or excels at. Most riders tackling something monumental like the Tevis have some sense of what they are doing, and have prepared their horse well. These aren't just horses; they are athletes. (To ride the Tevis, horses and riders must pass mileage qualification criteria.)

The death of Ice Joy was a tragedy, but neither his rider Skip (over 4000 endurance miles) nor Ice Joy (nearly 3000 endurance miles) were inexperienced. May Ice Joy rest in peace, and may Skip eventually get some peace.

There's no certain winning formula for finishing Tevis. The best horse and rider combination is not guaranteed a silver buckle. Although, if you study the two Tevis riders with the most Tevis buckles - Hal Hall, with 30 finishes in 36 starts, and Barbara White, with 34 finishes in 45 starts, through 2015 - you'll probably learn a thing or two.

And regarding experience on the Tevis trail, I am proof of the following points:

• Ignorance is not necessarily a bad thing. By being somewhat unenlightened about certain details, you spend a lot less time worrying about things - which really gets you nowhere anyway.

• Pre-riding the trail is not necessary for every rider and every horse. Some horses it may help, some it may not. I've heard stories both ways.

• Regarding pre-riding the cliff trails... do you *really* need to do that? I preferred to see them for the first time during Tevis, because the height wasn't going to change at all, and you just had to keep going anyway. I had and still have no need whatsoever to see what cliffs I rode over in the dark on the California loop.

• I was still prepared for Tevis, and so was my tough horse Quinn. Nance had him in top shape, and he had over 2000 AERC endurance miles. I had over 3000 miles. And though it was my first ride on Quinn, I believe that my experience helped me to read him and feel how he was feeling, and to ride him properly.

That said, though, what Tevis really is all about, in my opinion, is Luck. Luck plays a part in any outcome with horses, and Tevis Luck plays a huge part in every horse's and rider's result.

It was good luck that the unfamiliar saddle I rode in did not bother my knee at all - or else I'd have had serious problems. It was great luck that this was possibly one of the coolest Tevis Cups on record - or else I could have had serious problems. It was luck I was riding a horse that had completed Tevis already, who knew the trail and was unintimidated by anything, was fit, and that I got along with. It was luck I was riding with some people who knew the trail and the timing; I didn't have to worry about any of that. It was luck my horse didn't fall down when he tripped big time over that trail in the dark. It was luck we spent just exactly the right amount of time at vet checks. It was luck that we finished with 19 minutes left. It was luck we finished. The Tevis Gods were smiling on us that day and night.

On the other hand, someone bred a superior horse who would turn into an athlete and conquer the Tevis trail (twice). Someone (Nance) recognized his potential, and bought him and developed him into an athlete and rode him to that potential.

Everything about the ride was absolutely amazing. The trails were incredible. Just the thought of crossing the Sierra Nevadas on a horse, just like so many pioneers did 150 years ago, on some of those same trails, with the same views, some of the same difficulties, was awe inspiring.

The volunteers were unbelievable - there to help you

at every vet check/trot-by. "Food, water, hold your horse, do anything else for you?" There are 600 to 800 Tevis volunteers every year - a statistic that is in itself astonishing.

Friends were amazing: some showed up to cheer me on, some showed up at different crew spots to help us and other riders. It really does give a rider a mental lift.

My Idaho crew and fellow Idaho riders were utterly sensational - I couldn't, of course, have done it without them. I know now that I sure don't want to crew this ride, because it was a very stressful job for them (three crew members, five riders) - especially that first vet check at Robinson Flat! I wouldn't have known how fast to ride my borrowed horse; and of course I wouldn't have had a horse to ride in the first place without my munificent friend Nance. Quinn was all ready to go for Tevis, ready to just hop on... which is literally what I did. Got on him for the first time Friday for 30 minutes, and the second time Saturday for 100 miles. Nance is simply a wonderful, generous human being who enjoys sharing her love of endurance riding with friends.

And speaking of my horse Quinn: there are no words to aptly describe him. Nance had said, "Oh, he'll perk up when the sun goes down." He was never not energetic. Amazingly, he got stronger as the day went on. The power that was coming up from those legs, pounding over mile after mile after mile of challenging and demanding trail, was simply astounding.

It deserves to be said again that thanks go out to Tom who cancelled his ride and left a vacant saddle, to my guru Kevin and my hero Julie who absolutely had no doubts (like I did) about me riding and finishing, to my crew Bruce and Chris and Gentry, and excellent companion riders Nance, Kara, Laura and Chandler. And most of all, thanks to Nance, who just gave me this horse to ride, and to Quinn, who did it all. (Really - I just sat in the saddle.)

A couple of years have passed since the 2009 Tevis

Cup. I still pull out my silver Tevis buckle and look at it and think... Did I really ride in the Tevis? Did I really complete it? I still can't believe it.

I don't think I need to ride the Tevis again. I'm not obsessed with it, and this one ride was so magically perfect in every way. Anyway, the oldest Tevis finisher was 80 years old, so I have a couple decades to go yet before I seriously have to think about trying it again. Besides, I really am proud of my 100% Tevis completion rate. That may well have been 50% Luck and 50% Horse, but nevertheless, it's my Tevis record. I don't need to try to better it.

Then again, I have been offered a horse for another attempt...

11: **Tevis Tutorial**

(The week after Tevis)

by Tevis Expert Merri Melde (100% completions - 1 for 1)

Now that I'm an expert on the Tevis Cup and all, having a 100% completion rate (and I get extra points since I took almost the whole 24 hours, squeezing almost every minute out of it), I have prepared a tutorial for those who wish to complete the ride.

I was hoping to make it a big fat book that would end up at the top of the New York Times Best Seller list for months every year before July/August, but alas, it can be condensed and simplified into eight easy steps you can follow so that you, too, can complete Tevis and get your very own silver Tevis buckle.

1. Clever Sign-Up Timing - Don't make up your mind until Wednesday noon before the actual Tevis ride, and then pretend to fax your entry in to the Tevis office. Email them later and say, "I just faxed my entry to you, but only three of the pages went through. Then my fax machine broke before it sent page four (the one with my signature

of Release of Liability). Can I email you a photocopy of that page?" Jo-Anne from the Western States Trail Foundation will email you back, "We didn't get your fax. You can sign up Friday morning. Registration opens at 10 AM."

By doing it this way, you will have eliminated weeks, months, even years of worry, which does nothing for you in the way of boosting your confidence.

2. Heat Training - Pick just one day and spend five hours driving through Nevada on a hot day in July. To increase your discomfort, drive a car with no air conditioner, drive west so the sun hits you full on, and get stuck in road construction on I-80, facing westward into the hot sun. You might even, if you dare, wear black clothing to up the temperature just a smidge. Drive a car without a radio, which will intensify the effect of the heat, since there will be nothing to get your mind off the heat.

You will then be conditioned for the heat of those canyons that you will encounter in Tevis.

3. Physical Conditioning - If you aren't quite physically up to a hundred miler across the high and rugged Sierra Nevada mountain range, park your horse trailer and your horses as far as possible from the vet-in arena at Robie Park. That way, on Friday you will have to walk at least 17 times back and forth, hither and yon, at 7200 feet of altitude, between your trailer and camp central, to take photos, visit people, take photos, go to registration (twice), vet your horse in, visit more people all over camp, take more photos, pack your gear, shop at the vendors, take your horses for walks, visit with more people, etc.

You will then be in great physical shape for Tevis.

4. Weight Training - At Robie Park, at 7200 feet, carry two camera bags, two big cameras, a little camera, another little bag, and, preferably, a big cup of iced tea back and forth all day Friday while you are doing your physical conditioning.

You will then be strong enough to drag your weary butt up into the saddle one more time at mile 94 at approximately 3:31 AM, after approximately 22 hours and 16 minutes of riding. (You wondered where I got those times, right?)

5. Nerve Eradication - Pick a day where you set aside seven hours to do nothing but fret and worry about everything concerning Tevis: death (yours or your horse's), medical bills (yours or your horse's), the mortgage you are going to have to take out to do the ride (it's not cheap), the knee you might blow out (which means time lost riding), freak acts of nature (lightning storms, hailstorms, deep rivers, fires), the embarrassment you might feel if you do not finish (though, geez, just *entering* Tevis exempts you from that). While worrying about everything you can think of, and things you haven't, do not have any TV or radio on, don't talk to anybody on the phone; just sit there for seven hours and let yourself get nervous. (This, conveniently, can be done in tandem with your heat training, as you are driving across Nevada, in a car with no air conditioning or radio).

6. Preparedness - Approach the entire venture blindly. Do not do your homework. Do NOT pre-ride the Tevis trail. Stop reading stories about Cougar Rock and cliff trails and bees. Stop asking interview questions like, "What is the scariest part of the trail for you and why?" If you already asked this question several times, try to forget the answers, or at least don't look up on the trail map where they are. Stop recalling those stories you've heard over the years of horses falling off the trail (people too) and getting hurt or dying (not just during Tevis). Refuse to recall the time you yourself were packing with horses in the Sierra Nevadas just about 150 miles south of here, in the same terrain, where one of your pack horses flipped over backwards down a cliff and how you had to rescue him. Stop asking every rider what the temperature was at the bottom of the first canyon. Just stop asking questions, and

stop thinking about all of it.

7. Most important, have an amazing friend who has a good horse that is conditioned and ready, and who has already finished Tevis once, that she just GIVES you to ride.

8. And even more important - GO TO HAVE FUN! No matter who you are or who you are riding, you have a 50-50% chance of finishing. Why not enjoy the privilege and experience?

12: **Notes**

All the little extras you were wondering about...

Chapter 5:
Many of you are probably familiar with The Raven, who has travelled around the world with me and who has accompanied me on 8000+ miles of endurance riding. In fact, The Raven now has *two* Tevis buckles, and I only have one (he finished with Nick Warhol and Forever Dawn the next year.) But The Raven is a whole 'nother story in himself. He keeps a blog, Forevermore The Raven, at http://forevermoretheraven.blogspot.com/

Chapter 7:
Some people will "tail" a horse on foot - let the horse go in front of them and pull them up the hill. They'll hold onto the horse by a long lead line or long rein, and also hold onto the tail. It gives the horse a break from carrying the rider up the hills. And the rider has a little horsepower to pull him along uphill on foot.

Cougar Rock is where all those scenic, iconic Tevis pictures are taken, where the horses are lunging almost vertically upward over this gnarly mass of granite. You don't have to go up and over Cougar Rock (there's often a line, and horses have to go one at a time). There is a trail that goes around it. There are some breathtaking Youtube videos out there of horses clambering up and over Cougar Rock - look them up.

Cut-off times: Each vet check at Tevis has a cut-off time. If you do not arrive before the cut-off times, you're eliminated for Overtime, because it's been determined that if you are riding this slowly (even if it does not seem slow!), you will not be able to finish the ride.

Horses who passed the vet check at Robinson this year also had an exit exam before they went back out on trail, a quick check of their pulse and one more trot out.

Switching diagonals: if you were riding "properly" in an arena, you would post on the outside trotting diagonal. I automatically post on my "outside diagonal" with the curves in the trail. Switching diagonals keeps the horse more balanced as opposed to, say, posting on the same diagonal for 100 miles. Kind of like switching arms carrying a suitcase, instead of carrying it with one arm for 100 miles.

CRI: A horse's pulse is taken once, he is trotted by hand a certain distance and back, and his pulse is taken again one minute later. The second pulse should be lower than the first, like, say, 60-54. If not, it could be a sign that the horse is fatigued, particularly if the horse's pulse is already higher than 68.

Low gut sounds: The veterinarian listens to four quadrants of the gut, listening for sounds of movement/digestion. He should be able to hear something in all four quadrants. If not, it could possilby be a sign that all is not completely right with the horse. The veterinarian uses a number of parameters together to determine how the horse is doing, though the ultimate responsibility always, *always,* falls upon the rider.

Chapter 8:

Glowsticks on the breast collars: they give off a soft glow of light, presumably to help the horses to see a little better, though sometimes I think they are more of a comfort for humans! They are also often used by ride managers as trail markers for rides in the dark.

Chapter 9:

Red headlight: gives off a softer light and is presumably easier on horses' eyes in the dark.

The man and horse who went over the cliff were rescued in the morning. Horse was fine, man had broken his leg, but both were ultimately fine and returned to finish Tevis another year.

Sweep Riders of the Sierra (from their website): is an all-volunteer riding group established to provide safety and on-trail communications for endurance events on the Western States Trail and other Northern California locations. SOS Sweep Teams are composed of two to four riders that sweep one section of the trail before being relieved by a fresh team. Trail sections vary from six to 23 miles in length. Each team is responsible for following the last few competitors to assure that no one is lost or injured, while maintaining radio contact with "net control" at the finish line in Auburn.

Chapter 11:

I'm sure you realize the chapter title is ever so slightly facetious.

Random notes:

I still have my glass Tevis Guardian Angel. It did not break on the ride. I am saving it to pass on to the next special person riding Tevis.

Did I get sore from riding Tevis on an unfamiliar horse in an unfamiliar saddle? Oh my, yes. By noon-ish on Sunday, when I woke up from my nap, oh my, I could hardly walk. I limped and wobbled up to get my buckle from Julie Suhr (!!!!!!!!!) at the awards ceremony that afternoon, and in fact I limped and wobbled for a good three days afterwards (and riding home in the truck didn't help any!) And my eyes hurt for three days also. I went through two bottles of eyedrops. If I ever ride Tevis again (which I'm not planning on!) I will figure some way to wear goggles over my glasses.

ABOUT THE AUTHOR

Merri Melde, a.k.a. The Equestrian Vagabond, is a horse photographer, writer, author, photojournalist, artist, horse packer, carriage driver, racetrack groom, spotted owl hooter, wildlife technician, Raven fanatic, trail builder, sound engineer, theatre techie, world traveler, clawhammer banjo player, owner of The Most Beautiful Horse On The Planet (Stormy), rabid obsessed endurance rider, and Tevis Cup finisher. But not all at the same time.

Merri has written for over a dozen magazines, and photographed for over two dozen magazines around the world, and traveled in over three dozen countries, sometimes seeking adventure and enlightenment, and often chasing horses.

She's the author of *Soul Deep in Horses: Memoir of an Equestrian Vagabond, Tevis Cup Magic: Taking on the World's Toughest 100 Mile Endurance Ride*, and the short stories, *Traveler Tales,* and *Racehorse Tales,* available on Amazon.com.

THANK YOU READER!

Thank you for reading! If you loved reading this book (or any of my others), please consider leaving a review on Amazon.com. And I love hearing your comments. You can drop me a line at theequestrianvagabond.com .

If you loved this story, you will love my book *Soul Deep in Horses: Memoir of an Equestrian Vagabond*. It's available on Amazon as a softcover book, and as an ebook (it's also iTunes/iPad/iTouch and Kobo).

Tevis Cup Magic is also available as an ebook on Amazon.com.

Also check out my website, www.TheEquestrian.com, for jaw-dropping equine photography, unique handmade horse art, and other fun stuff. For more adventurous horse stories and photos, you can follow my blog at http://theequestrianvagabond.blogspot.com/ .

www.teviscup.org has all the Tevis info you need to know to qualify and sign up for the Tevis.

www.aerc.org has all the info you need to get started in endurance riding, so you can start planning on your own Tevis Cup!

www.endurance.net reports on endurance rides around the USA and around the world.

Happy Trails!

Made in the USA
Columbia, SC
24 March 2019